Executive Summary

Many Americans today have lost faith in the U.S. government and see specifically the Federal Bureau of Investigation (FBI) as threatening them as opposed to protecting them. Many Americans, the author included, are deeply concerned about potential government overreach and threats to our liberty and freedom, specifically regarding the 1st and 2nd Amendments of the constitution. Unlike the vast majority of those who have lost faith in the government, the author has not, and this report was compiled to help frame the correct conversation, one not driven by political rhetoric or motivated by bureaucratic distortions. The author believes, if we can have this conversation, we can avoid disaster.

This Critical Report is the authors own personal opinions and analysis based on many years of experience in intelligence collection, analysis, targeting and strategic military planning. This Critical Report is also based on having information from having been on the inside of the conversation regarding domestic violent extremism and domestic terrorism policy while working at the Office of the Director of National Intelligence (ODNI) in the National Counterterrorism Center (NCTC) and serving as the Senior Collection Strategist on Domestic Terrorism. The author had direct access to everything the FBI had in its holding regarding domestic extremism and drafted the national strategy for intelligence collection on domestic extremists intended for the National Security Council.

This report was written specifically to help the American people understand the current domestic terrorism conversation going on in the U.S. government and to arm our political leaders with the information they need to combat the real problem.

This Critical Report was compiled from public statements made by government officials, official government documents, outside organizations who are trusted authoritative voices as well as publicly available information, including some leaked information specific to the issue of domestic terrorism and extremism. This report was approved for release by the Office of the Director of National Intelligence with redactions.

Key Findings

The FBI claims that international and domestic terrorism are the FBI's #1 priority and that domestic terrorists (specifically lone actor white supremists and militia extremists) pose a greater threat today than do international terrorist organizations. The FBI claims domestic terrorism is metastasizing and not going away any time soon.

- Available data refutes these claims.
- The most significant motivation to violence is mental health problems. Anxiety, depression, hopelessness, and a search for meaning in their life often times exasperated by loss of faith in the U.S. government as well as conspiracy theories and foreign influence.
- During the National Counterterrorism Center - Domestic Terrorism Conference of 2020 the FBI made it clear regarding its desire to circumvent the constitution and their desire to designate groups in the U.S. as domestic terrorist organizations despite the constitution.
- Fear of government overreach and threats to the U.S. Constitution are exacerbated by the FBIs eagerness to ignore the constitution and their unwillingness to accept responsibility for their mistakes.
- The FBI understands the threat of "domestic terrorism" is exaggerated by politicians and the media but the FBI benefits from the exaggerated threat by being granted expanded authorities and increased budget.
- The FBI claims that the threat posed by lone actor white supremists and militia extremists is worse than the range of other cyber threats, nation state threats, criminal organizations such as MS-13, violence toward law enforcement and the vast unrelenting counterintelligence threat from China.
- The FBIs plan is to recruit more Americans to spy on their fellow Americans and arrest more Americans in-order-to understand the "tradecraft" being used by potential domestic extremists to conceal their activities.
- **(redacted)** If true, then FBI agents conducting investigations are deliberately falsifying investigative records to continue an investigation in hopes of a prosecution.
- The Directors of both the FBI and DHS are aware the problem is a mental health problem, but they deliberately mislead our political leaders and the American people in-order-to expand their authorities and increase their agency budgets.

The FBI uses a handling cavate, Law Enforcement Sensitive (LES), to keep the FBI's true understanding of the threat out of the hands of the American people and our elected officials indefinitely. There is no release date for LES. Only about 2% of FBI reporting regarding domestic extremists and terrorism is Secret or Top Secret. 98% of FBI reporting on domestic extremists is Unclassified//LES.

- The author contends that LES is being used by the FBI to avoid unwanted scrutiny as well as "conceal violations of law, inefficiency, or administrative error, to prevent embarrassment to a person, organization, or agency." And is in violation of federal regulations regarding the classification of government information.
- In 2009 a DHS Assessment was "leaked." Titled, (redacted), the key findings of which were very interesting including the threats to America supposedly posed by (redacted)
- (redacted) This assessment could very easily have been stated this way: Many Americans who believe in the U.S. Constitution will not take kindly to threats to the U.S. Constitution. Supposedly, those people who believe in the constitutional right to bear arms, as written in the constitution and who have served the country in the military pose a threat to America and are probably racists.
- According to the assessment of the DHS and the FBI the supposed causes of the increase in domestic extremism where: (redacted)

The FBI claims they will be able to protect America from lone actors motivated to violence if they have a domestic terrorism federal statute needed to circumvent the 1st Amendment of the constitution. The 1st Amendment was written specifically to prohibit the federal government doing these things. Important documents drafted by the author raising this concern were never forwarded to the National Security Council.

- The FBI believes the 1st Amendment of the constitution should be viewed as a "factor, not a constraint."
- The FBI believes a domestic terrorism federal statute might be useful "for deterrence purposes and provide additional federal violation to authorize predication of an investigation."
- A recent listing of threats by the FBI were domestic terrorists first, foreign motivated terrorists second, election security third, citizens access to encryption forth, China fifth, and cyber sixth. But the FBI has very little involvement in most of these issues. This listing highlights the FBIs agenda to use a domestic terrorism statute to threaten Americans free speech as well as privacy.

There has been a significant loss of faith and trust in the U.S. Government going back to the 1950s but in particular recently, after the unconstitutional investigations of Michael Flynn, (redacted) and the fabricated counterintelligence investigation against candidate Donald Trump which the FBI tried to cover up. Lack of government transparency when the FBI commit these acts and are caught, leads to many of the false narratives, conspiracy theories, and supposed "extremist" rhetoric from people who demand the law enforcement communities, and our political leaders abide by the U.S. Constitution.

- Failures in transparency with the America people (Ruby Ridge 1992, Waco – 1993, unconstitutional investigations and violations of Americans civil liberties drive Americans to distrust the FBI) giving rise to the distrust of the American people.
- The FBI has a long history of constitutional abuses going back to the 1950s such as the COINTELPRO Counterintelligence Program which the Church Committee of the U.S. Senate (spying on American citizens in groups ranging from the Ku Klux Klan, the Socialist Workers Party, and the Black Panther Party, Martin Luther King and more recently former President Donald Trump, General Michael Flynn, Carter Paige and The Make America Great Again Movement or Patriot Movement).
- This has been particularly exasperated by the case against Gen Michael Flynn, as well as what happened to (redacted). These types of counterintelligence operations are common however (redacted) Falsifying FISA warrants and internal documents to maintain illegal investigations is not.

- The Director of DHS recently begun a review of the employees of DHS in order to remove threats of domestic extremism from the organization. However, the extremists he is proposing to purge are Americans who fervently believe in the U.S. Constitution. Every American should be demanding to know what the criteria is for the "review." Anyone who does not "get in line" will be purged.

The FBI is not interested in stopping threats because they are focused on getting prosecutions and have a long history of problems administering their Criminal Informant Program which is the current primary source of information regarding suppose "domestic extremists."

- Confidential human sources motivated by money or avoiding incarceration (judicial coercion) leads to problems with the reliability of the information collected and may cause these individuals to encourage or facilitate extremists or exaggerate or falsify their reports to the FBI.
- **(UPDATE 17 November 2021)** According to the 2019 Office of the Inspector General's November 2019 Audit of the Federal Bureau of Investigation's Management of its Confidential Human Source Validation Processes; the FBI's CHS program does not comply with their own policies, DOJ policy or the IC policy regarding validation of human sources, especially high risk long-term CHS, to such a degree that it can not be considered an intelligence organization.
- **(UPDATE 17 November 2021)** Those responsible for the validation process are untrained, the data bases housing the CHS information is inadequate, and the validation personnel are instructed not to document any derogatory information regarding a source during a review that would interfere with using the source in court.
- **(UPDATE 17 November 2021)** The activities of the validation personnel as well as the agents make the discovery responsibilities for prosecutors impossible. This FBI policy is done deliberately to prevent information from being discoverable by criminal suspects in their defense.
- **(UPDATE 17 November 2021)** There is no oversight of CHS operations except for the field office review with regard to CHS operations.

The FBI does not explore the possibility of Black Swan (events that are completely impossible to predict) events or conduct Red-Teaming activities to explore possible threats. Such things like what happened in Kenosha, Wisconsin and in Washington, DC on January 6th for example. These types of exercises are common in the intelligence community however **(redacted)**

According to the U.S. Senate report on the January 6th Rally at the Capital, the reasons for the breach of the Capitol was everyone's else's fault except the political leaders themselves.

- There was no mention in the report of the incredible tensions created in the country regarding legitimate concerns by many Americans of threats to election security which even the director of the FBI has stated is a priority.
- The real blame falls on the politicians for feeding the anxiety of the American people on both sides of the ideological spectrum.
- The real blame lies with the media who pretend to report the news but prey on people's fears for profit.

Recommended Solutions

- **True Faith and Allegiance to the U.S. Constitution:** Our political leaders and every member of the DHS and the FBI have sworn oaths to uphold the constitution. If we just accepted that the constitution protects all free speech, even speech you do not like, and that law-abiding citizens should not be worried about gun confiscation because owning firearms is an unalienable right, this would go a long way to setting this issue.

- **We don't have a domestic terrorism problem. We have a mental health problem:** We do not have a white supremacy problem or an anti-government problem or a militia problem. The data cannot be denied in comparison to the suicide problem, the opioids problem, the homelessness problem, the inner-city gang violence problem, or the fatherlessness problem. No domestic threat to America today is worse than the mental health problem that leads to many of these other problems. A whole-of-government approach to mental health care must be created to address this problem. A domestic terrorism federal statute, expanded FBI authorities to violate the constitutional rights of American citizens, continued rhetoric by politicians about taking away their guns, will have absolutely no impact on the myriad of other much more significant threats we face and would likely only intensify the problem.

- **Transparency:** Complete transparency with the American people is the only possible solution to regaining the trust and faith of the American people. There is an increasing amount of distrust among the American people because of legitimate concerns about the threats to their liberty by the very government claiming to protect them. It is clear the FBI wants a domestic terrorism federal statute to circumvent the 1st Amendment. When the FBI or any part of the U.S. government screws up and tries to cover it up, this only aggravates the distrust. The vast majority of FBI personnel are moral, ethical, and loyal guardians of the constitution. But this is not how they are perceived from the outside by many regular Americans who just love our country and the constitution. The 2020 Domestic Terrorism Conference highlighted transparency as a concern when they recommended: "The U.S. Government needs to find a way to increase public trust by being transparent with the public about how DT definitions are derived, defined, and used; and We (the U.S. government) can undermine the public trust by failing to be transparent or clear about terms—how the U.S. Government uses terms, what we mean by them, and how that may differ from the public's intuitive understanding of DT."

Conclusion

Many Americans today still believe America is the greatest country that has ever existed in the history of mankind, and many are willing to do whatever it takes to protect it from all enemies foreign and domestic. If believing that makes us extremists, then I guess we are.

This report was written specifically to help the American people understand the current domestic terrorism conversation going on in the U.S. government from someone formerly on the inside and to arm our political leaders with the information they need to combat the misinformation which abounds.

To my fellow intelligence professionals out there and the members of the FBI, DHS, CIA, NSA, NRO etc. I apologize for the production quality of this report, but I did not have my brothers and sisters to rely upon to proof it. I believed getting it out to the public and into the hands of our political leaders was more important than the formatting.

I know it is hard but if you have the courage to do so, please join with me in helping preserve this great country. Now is the time for us to stand up and speak truth to power. Now is the time.

Your humble servant,

Tom Speciale
American

What is a Collection Strategist?

In October 2020, I accepted a contract position in the Office of the Director of National Intelligence (ODNI) National Counterterrorism Center (NCTC) serving as the Senior Collection Strategist on Domestic Terrorism. You will know if you have read my autobiography, *Faith, Family and Fortitude: Seeing Opportunities Instead of Obstacles*, I had worked in this office before.

The last time I worked at NCTC, I was forced to leave the contract because my government supervisor was altering intelligence information in a way that I felt was misleading the Obama Administration and the National Security Council regarding the intelligence collection capabilities and clandestine operations of various agencies.

My focus during this new contract was to draft the (redacted) which served as the document addressing the intelligence communities understanding of our capabilities and obstacles specifically regarding collection on domestic extremists. The assembly of this highly classified information is simple, you send out a request across the IC and law enforcement and ask them all to answer some questions regarding their capabilities and limitations to collecting intelligence on a specific threat. They respond individually and then as the Collection Strategist you put this entire document together and get it approved by leadership and then ultimately it goes to the National Security Council and senior leadership across the IC so they will better understand our capabilities, limitations, and gaps in collection on that topic or threat.

Secondly, my job was to draft a (redacted) A CPS is a document which goes out across the intelligence collection community to highlight intelligence gaps and articulate important intelligence questions the community has regarding a particular threat. In this case, racially and ethnically motivated violent extremists. (redacted)

What is Domestic Terrorism?

As a senior intelligence analyst and counterterrorism expert since 2010 I had access to the NCTC website for many years and had daily stayed abreast of the most relevant reporting regarding terrorism. I stayed on top of these reports as part of my regular responsibilities. Most of the terrorism reporting was related to overseas terrorists or what are called Homegrown Violent Extremists (HVEs), Americans who become radicalized to carry out attacks in the U.S. in support of foreign ideologies, principally ISIS, Al Qaida etc.

Over the last year or two there had been a trickle of domestic terrorism reporting on racially or ethnically motivated violent extremists (REMVE), as well as anti-government, militia extremists etc. The FBI for some reason most often just says RMVE, dropping the ethnic elements used by the intelligence community. These reports over the years were almost universally after-the-fact reports concerning domestic and overseas extremists who had carried out some horrible attack against their preferred target of animosity.

In the last few years there were also a few reports of INCELs (Involuntary Celibates), young men who are frustrated with their inability to meet and have relationships with women and who become so angry at society they carry out high-profile attacks targeting women to make a name for themselves. These young men were also almost universally suffering from major mental health issues. But what I thought was interesting was that the mental health of many of these individuals was never mentioned in intelligence reporting.

Thus, for several years I had been reading intelligence reporting on known or suspected domestic extremists. But what became clear to me over time was "domestic terrorists" were rarely if ever organized. They had no unifying ideology although they might profess similar grievances. They might belong to likeminded groups, but it was extremely rare to be able to get more than one or two to carry out any kind of "terror attack" with the purpose of causing a political change.

In almost every case, these attacks were carried out by lone actors who carried out an attack because they were otherwise living a completely meaningless life. In their minds, they were nothing, nobody, meaningless. No one would even know they had even lived unless they did these horrible things.

The advent of social media had become a major contributor to their belief that they would become famous. The normal trajectory for these young men, was they were very often anti-social, suffering from mental health issues such as anxiety, depression or in some cases autism, they had few friends and limited or inadequate support from families.

It was my belief, based on all the intelligence reporting I was reading, as well as the outside research I was doing on gun violence, suicide and inner-city violent crime that what we were experiencing was a mental health crisis not a domestic extremism not a domestic terrorism crisis. Some of these lone actors were even motivated to violence because they had engaged with similarly minded people through social media and were often goaded into carrying out attacks to achieve some sense of meaning in their otherwise meaningless lives.

In the case of the racial and ethnically motivated extremists (REMVEs) who became motivated to violence, they too were quite often anti-social and suffered from anxiety and depression as well as in many cases suffering from other psychological and mental health issues. Those motivated to violence were motivated I believed by the same reasons INCELs are motivated to violence – looking for meaning and purpose in an otherwise meaningless life.

For many of these people, that meaning, or purpose might be the illusion they will kick off a race war. But the actual cause was their state of mind, their mental health, their lack of a support system in their lives, not racism. Hatred and racism are just the excuse in their meaningless lives.

I also noted another problem fueling the violence. Possibly even more concerning than their mental health. Many of those motivated to violence had lost their faith in their government or believed that the U.S. government was becoming less and less interested in protecting people's civil rights of free speech or the right to protect themselves. Essentially, more and more Americans were feeling as though the government was "threatening" them. They were feeling more and more that they needed to protect themselves from the government. These thoughts or feelings might in fact be the only thing that made them unique or gave them purpose.

Our Federal Government and Domestic Terrorism

- **Ruby Ridge - 1992**

Ruby Ridge was the location of a violent 11-day standoff with federal authorities in remote Boundary County, Idaho, beginning in late August of 1992. U.S. Marshals and federal agents faced off against Randy Weaver, his wife and five children and his friend Kevin Harris. The Ruby Ridge incident was the culmination of years of investigation into Weaver by local authorities, the FBI, the ATF, and the Secret Service. It ended with the shooting deaths of a U.S. Marshal, Weaver's wife Vicki and their teenage son Samuel (Sammy). It was an absolute fiasco and ultimately Randy Weaver was paid 3.1 million dollars for the deaths of his wife and child.[1]

- Waco, Texas - 1993

The Waco crisis started when the ATF raided a religious compound based on reports of federal firearms violations. Clearly this was a 1st and 2nd Amendment issue. The Branch Davidian's were an apocalyptic cult awaiting the collapse of the world, believing the Bible was the literal word of God, and looked to the Bible for clues about the end of the world and Christ's Second Coming. It should not come as a surprise to anyone that the cultists believed when the FBI and ATF surrounded their compound this was in fact the end of days for them and decided to defend themselves. Four ATF agents and six Branch Davidians died in the initial shootout.[2]

This was followed by a 51-day siege of the Branch Dividian compound by 900 law enforcement officials. In an effort to "negotiate" with the cultists the federal government used ear-splitting loud music focused on the compound and destroyed their vehicles by crushing them with tanks.[3]

This does not sound like a particularly effective negotiation tactic when dealing with a group of religious radicals who preach that the government is going to come someday and kill them.

Just after 6 a.m. on April 19, 1993, FBI agents used two tanks to "penetrate" the compound and deposit approximately 400 containers of CS gas inside the building. Seventy-six people died when the building caught on fire, including 25 children.[4]

It took years to get to the truth of what happened in Waco. The U.S. government covered up the fact that they had essentially murdered 76 people including 25 children while "trying to save them."[5] For years, the U.S. government covered up their mistakes in the handling of this situation fueling the rise of militias and anti-government groups around the country.[6] Fueling the rise of the distrust of federal law enforcement.

The federal government later was forced to admit that there was no evidence of child abuse going on in the compound which had been used as the justification for the raid and the ordering of the gas attack which was determined (in 1999) to have started the fire.[7][8]

But before the truth came out regarding both Ruby Ridge and Waco, Texas, in April 1995 on the second anniversary of the Waco siege's end, an Army veteran named Timothy McVeigh used a truck loaded with 4,800 pounds of fuel oil and aluminum nitrate to blow up the Alfred P. Murrah Federal Building in Oklahoma City, Oklahoma. With a total of 168 people killed and some 850 wounded, the Oklahoma City bombing is by far the deadliest domestic terrorist attack in the United States to date.[9] I believe this is one of very few true domestic terrorist attacks because it was carried out against the government with an intent of forcing change in the government.

There are more of these types of incidents where the federal government has violated citizens civil liberties like Waco and Ruby Ridge, but these are some of the most egregious and the most motivational for Americans to have lost trust in the FBI as well as other federal law enforcement agencies.

I propose if the U.S. government owned their mistakes regarding Waco and Ruby Ridge earlier they would have maintained the faith and trust of American citizens and Timothy McVeigh may not have blown up the Murrah Building. McVeigh specifically said that it was because of these events he had carried out his attack.[10] His attack is in no way justified. But it does meet the criteria of a domestic terrorist attack to bring about change in government and I believe had the government been transparent about their mistakes it may not have occurred at all.

Do we really have a domestic terrorist problem in the U.S. today?

According to a ProPublica article from January 7th, 2021 – "federal authorities have had more success combating international terrorists than those with a domestic focus, reflecting <u>legal limits on investigations of American political groups, the opaque and elusive nature of the threat, and President Donald Trump's embrace of far-right groups</u>, experts say."[11]

This sounds like a direct equivalency being drawn between jihadist organizations and President Trump. What could the author mean by "legal limits to investigate American political groups" or "opaque nature of the threat?"[12]

So, the "legal limitations" are the constitution. The "opaque and elusive nature of the threat" is the fact that they are almost universally lone actors motivated by deep personal grievances or most often people who are mentally ill which I am pretty sure is not the prerogative of federal law enforcement. The fact that the FBI would say President Trump's "embrace of far-right groups" is the FBI's way of saying racism, anti-government and INCEL extremists are President Trump's fault. That is imbecilic. These supposed "threats" have been here for centuries.

The article goes on to say, "One fundamental problem is that while federal statutes provide a definition of domestic terrorism, there is not a specific law outlawing it."[13]

In his opening remarks Michael McGarrity, The FBI Counterterrorism Division Assistant Director stated on June 4th, 2019, presented the FBIs talking points regarding domestic terrorism in a House hearing. As I was watching this, I was reminded that when speaking before the House and Senate these individuals swear to tell the truth - the whole truth. [14]

I do not think they are telling us the whole truth. In fact, I know they are not telling us the **whole** truth.

According to Michael McGarrity the FBI's number 1 priority is international and domestic terrorism. We must assume then that these two things pose the most existential threat to America if they are the number 1 priority. He goes on to say that this domestic terrorism threat is a "white supremacy, anti-government and anti-authority" threat. [15]

According to McGarrity, "Domestic terrorists are Americans who commit violent criminal acts in the furtherance of ideological goals stemming from domestic influence such as bias, racial bias, and anti-government sentiment." He tells us how bad this threat is by saying, "We assess domestic terrorists pose a persistent and evolving threat of violence and economic harm to the United States; in fact, there have been more domestic terrorism subjects disrupted by arrest and more deaths caused by domestic terrorists than international terrorists in recent years."[16]

Further he says, "We are most concerned about lone offenders, primarily using firearms, as these lone offenders represent the dominant trend for lethal domestic terrorists. Frequently, these individuals act without a clear group affiliation or guidance, making them challenging to identify, investigate, and disrupt."[17]

Further he says, "We understand that your request for today's hearing arises from a concern about racially motivated violent extremism, which may result in the commission of hate crimes. We appreciate your interest in this issue. Individuals adhering to racially motivated violent extremism ideology have been responsible for the most lethal incidents among domestic terrorists in recent years, and the FBI assesses the threat of violence and lethality posed by racially motivated violent extremists will continue. The current racially motivated violent extremist threat is decentralized and primarily characterized by lone actors. These actors tend to be radicalized online and target minorities and soft targets using easily accessible weapons."[18]

McGarrity states matter of fact, that the FBI's number one priority is stopping "terrorists" - lone actors, using firearms and operating without any connection to a leadership hierarchy or group and radicalization occurs in isolation and on-line. "Sometimes this presents mitigation difficulties."[19]

Supposedly, according to the FBI, domestic terrorism is the number one threat posed to the United States. "In 2018 domestic violent extremists conducted six lethal attacks killing seventeen victims. In 2017 domestic violent extremists conducted five lethal attacks killing eight victims." And "In fact, many arrests of FBI domestic terrorism subjects are conducted by state and local partners." "In fiscal year 2018, FBI Joint Terrorism Task Force across the country proactively arrested approximately 115 subjects of FBI domestic terrorism investigations before they could mobilize to violence."[20]

- **What the FBI really wants.**

If you really want to understand this issue, and why the FBI is struggles with domestic intelligence activities, go watch the back and forth between Rep. Alexandria Ocasio-Cortez and Asst. Director McGarrity in the House hearing. What Rep. Ocasio-Cortez is struggling to understand is the differences between foreign inspired attacks and domestically inspired attacks.[21]

When asked "Is white supremacy not a global issue?" Asst. Director McGarrity replies, "It is a global issue." When asked, "So why are they not charged with foreign...." Asst. Director McGarrity explains, "Because the United States Congress does not have a statute for us for domestic terrorism like we do on a foreign terrorist organization like ISIS, al Qaeda, Al Shabab." [22]

Michael McGarrity, makes clear that the reason Americans are not charged with domestic terrorism, "There is no domestic terrorism charge like 18 U.S. Code § 2339 A, B, C, D for foreign terrorist organizations."[23]

The real answer is much simpler. This is America.

People are free to think whatever they want in America. If they commit a criminal act, then they can and should be prosecuted.

But despite this, the FBI believes having such a statue, a domestic terrorism federal statute, would give them the ability to stop "domestic terrorists" by having a legal statute allowing the FBI to circumvent the U.S. Constitution.

> **Note:** For more information on the Foreign Federal Terrorism Stature see: § 2339. Harboring or concealing terrorists; § 2339A. Providing material support to terrorists; § 2339B. Providing material support or resources to designated foreign terrorist organizations; § 2339C. Prohibitions against the financing of terrorism; § 2339D. Receiving military-type training from a foreign terrorist organization.

Supposedly the FBI would be able to use this statute to "protect us" by collecting intelligence on American citizens who have views someone (Who exactly we don't know) believes are radical or extreme and potentially violence or criminal. The funny thing is - this is the exact reason for the 1st Amendment. It was written specifically to limit the government from doing this.

The "domestic terrorist" claim by the FBI was not new. Most of what every day people think of as domestic terrorism or hate speech is, and always has been, constitutionally protected free speech. It might be despicable and hateful, but it is legal.

There are many things said today that I find despicable and hateful and ignorant on both sides of the conversation about racism, abortion, illegal immigrants, gay people, white people, black people, brown people, Asian people etc. etc. However, when it comes to supposed domestic terrorist attacks, I know the actual threat is most often lone actors carrying out violent attacks with little indication or warning other than their mental health problems making it a local law enforcement issue or a medical health care issue not a federal law enforcement issue.

There is no federal statute for domestic terrorism for the above reasons. Domestic extremists of all stripes are regularly prosecuted for other crimes such as possessing or using illegal firearms or making illegal weapons like explosives or planning attacks. The legal challenges to use the same intelligence capabilities we use against foreign threats against U.S. persons would be hindered by that pesky thing we call a constitution.

The legal authorities governing organizations like CIA, NSA, DoD etc. make it impossible for them to become actively involved in domestic intelligence activities except in instances where there is a foreign nexus. I knew all of this before I took the NCTC job as the Senior Collection Strategist for Domestic Terrorists because I knew what Executive Order 12333 and the U.S. Constitution said.

According to Executive Order 12333--United States intelligence activities regarding collection activities states: "Agencies within the Intelligence Community shall use the least intrusive collection techniques feasible within the United States or directed against United States persons abroad. Agencies are not authorized to use such techniques as electronic surveillance, unconsented physical search, mail surveillance, physical surveillance, or monitoring devices unless they are in accordance with procedures established by the head of the agency concerned and approved by the Attorney General. Such procedures shall protect constitutional and other legal rights and limit use of such information to lawful governmental purposes."[24]

As it applies to counterintelligence activities covered in Executive Order (EO) 12333 – "Counterintelligence means information gathered and activities conducted to protect against espionage, other intelligence activities, sabotage, or assassinations conducted for or on behalf of foreign powers, organizations or persons, or international terrorist activities, but not including personnel, physical, document or communications security programs."[25]

So, the only way you can lawfully conduct a CI investigation is if you have reason to believe the individual or individuals are working for a foreign power or designated foreign terrorist group.

Some really great work has been done in the last few years by the Center for Strategic and International Studies on domestic extremist terrorism. Two reports are of interest on this topic: *The War Comes Home – The Evolution of Domestic Terrorism in the United States* by Seth Jones, Catrina Doxsee, Nicholas Harrington, Grace Hwang, and James Suber in October 2020 and *The Military, Police, and the Rise of Terrorism in the United States* by Jones, Doxsee, Hwang and Jared Thompson from April 2021.

- What the data says.

In the first brief, CSIS points out that while there seems to be an increase in the number of attacks by white supremacists, anarchists, and anti-fascists as well as other types of extremists the number of fatalities is relatively low compared to previous years. CSIS points out that while the FBI and DHS claim that these ideologies or hate groups "remain the most persistent and lethal threat in the Homeland," they provide no data to support this claim. CSIS relied on publicly available data going back to 1994 to construct their data sets. [26]

According to CSIS, "The number of fatalities from terrorist attacks in the U.S. homeland is still relatively small compared to some periods in U.S. history, making it important not to overstate the threat. Roughly half of the years since 1994 had a greater number of fatalities from terrorism than 2020—at least between January 1 and August 31, 2020."

An interesting point that CSIS makes is that they do not count hate crimes or hate speech as domestic terrorism. Leading one to believe that maybe we should all try and get on the same sheet of music regarding what domestic terrorism is. Does the FBI lump graffiti and "verbal abuse" in with physical violence? If so, are they doing so to inflate their numbers to make a bigger problem out of this than it is? Additionally, the CSIS research did not include "protests, looting, and broader civil disturbances." [27]

CSIS identified 61 incidents that occurred in the U.S. between January 1 and August 31, 2020. Of those 41 were identified as far-right violence, 12 as far-left violence, and four each of Salafist-Jihadi or "other." [28]

The only concern I have regarding the data provided in the CSIS report is that they rely on percentages rather than the raw figures. This is a common problem when looking at data, because the raw numbers of events are more revealing in my opinion.

For example, one of the CSIS data pie charts tell us that 50% of violent far-right attacks targeted demonstrators. So how many is that? Of the 41 far-right attacks three did not have identified targets, leaving 38. So, we must figure out for ourselves that about 20 or 21 attacks were directed against demonstrators, 1 was abortion related, 1 was against a religious institution, 1 was against transportation and infrastructure, 1 against the media, 6 were against private individuals, 6 against the government, military, or police and 1 against "other." On the other hand of the 20 far-left attacks about 12 were against government, military, or police and 8 against demonstrators. [29] In a free society of over 350 million people, made of people from all over the world, 61 incidents seem like an exceptionally low number.

What does this tell us? I like how CSIS assessed the data – "The rise in violent far-left and far-right attacks against demonstrators may have been caused by the emerging security dilemma in urban areas, where there was a combustible mix of large crowds, angry demonstrators, and weapons." [30]

Although I disagree with including weapons in the "combustible mix." Anything can and will be used as a weapon – bricks, sticks, automobiles etc. and in fact are. Over five times as many people die from "fists and feet" than do rifles, all rifles, in the U.S., every year. Maybe we really should confiscate all the "assault feet" Americans have access to.

So, how bad is it actually? According to CSIS data, "Despite the large number of terrorist incidents, there were only five fatalities caused by domestic terrorism in the first eight months of 2020. There were four times as many far-left terrorist incidents and the same number of far-right terrorist incidents in 2020 as in all of 2019. Yet only 5 of the 61 incidents (8 percent) recorded between January and August 2020 resulted in fatalities, excluding the perpetrator." [31] And, "the number of fatalities in 2020 was low compared to the past five years, in which total fatalities ranged from 22 to 66 fatalities." [32]

So, five. Five fatalities in 2020 from January to August. Does this sound to you like it should be the FBIs number one priority?

These events get a lot of attention in the media, but they don't amount to much in the grand scheme of things. And certainly, 5 deaths are not going to bring about a political change.

I highly recommend everyone read the offered "Future Developments" section in the CSIS brief pre-January 6th, 2021. It is important to see what they were thinking would be potential threats after the 2020 election.

What I believe is missing from overall domestic terrorism conversation is the fact that the mental health crisis in the U.S. is in great measure a critical component to the perceived domestic terrorism threat.

Also, the missing component of loss of faith in the U.S. government for their past violations against American citizens civil liberties – Waco, Ruby Ridge, Martin Luther King, Michael Flynn, Carter Paige etc. The lack of transparency about their mistakes leading to the increased distrust. Nor does the article mention the foreign exacerbation of the division in the U.S. by foreign actors such as Russia, China, and Iran.

I believe that these three components are the real cause of the rise in domestic extremism and the associated violence. This hyper-rhetoric is also being fueled by politicians and government agencies who fear admitting their mistakes, as well as by foreign government organizations who are dedicated to our downfall. The intelligence community, the actual intelligence community, CIA, NSA, NGA, NRO, etc. all know this, and they are reporting it. Why doesn't the FBI seem to understand or worse refuse to listen?

- **The threat posed by veterans.**

The second brief published by CSIS, *The Military, Police, and the Rise of Terrorism in the United States* by Jones, Doxsee, Hwang and Jared Thompson from April 2021 is also important to understand the level of participation of active duty and reservists in supposed domestic extremism and terrorism. According to CSIS research there was a rise in active duty and reservist involvement. This is especially concerning to me because I am a reserve Army Warrant Officer.

According to CSIS active duty and reservist involvement rose from 1.5% to 6.4%. This is misleading. Here are the actual numbers from CSIS: "The percentage of attacks and plots committed by active-duty and reserve personnel rose in 2020 to 6.4 percent of all attacks and plots (7 of 110 total), up from 1.5 percent in 2019 (1 of 65 total) and none in 2018. Active-duty personnel perpetrated 4.5 percent of the attacks in 2020 (five incidents), and reservists conducted 1.8 percent (two incidents)."[33] CSIS admits that this is a tiny percentage of all current active duty and reservist personnel.

One, one service member, is too many for me. But again, there is no mention of other factors such as mental health. I believe that since military personnel swear an oath to defend the constitution, it should stand to reason that more and more military personnel would be retaliating against a government they have lost faith in. I am not excusing the behavior. I am trying to point out that the government needs to do better regarding owning their mistakes if they want to have faith and trust from the American people.

- **Are there extremists in the military?**

The CSIS brief points out, "In 2020, the FBI alerted the DoD that it had opened 143 criminal investigations involving current or former service members—of which nearly half (68) were related to domestic extremism. Most investigations apparently involved veterans, some of whom had unfavorable discharge records. The January 6, 2021, events at the U.S. Capitol raised additional concerns, since one reservist, one National Guard member, and at least 31 veterans were charged with conspiracy or other crimes." [34]

We do not know yet how many of those charged will be convicted but I will tell you that I was investigated just for being at the Capital on the 6th of January. I assure you I was not involved in any conspiracy or any other crime, but I know through my chain of command that members of the military did interview my current and past commander to determine if I had any extremist ideological tendencies.

But, I have yet to hear anything from either the FBI or the DoD at the time of this writing. I must tell you that it makes me incredibly sad that I, someone who has devoted my life to my country since I was 18 (1987), am considered a possible extremist just for attending a political rally, which I am sure is protected in the constitution.

I also spoke at the rally, which I am sure is also protected activity. I voiced my concerns about the government, which I am sure is Constitutionally protected activity. I even followed the rules of not presenting myself as a spokesman for the Department of Defense or the Army Reserves because that would not have been why I was there. My heart aches at the thought someone could even consider this about me or any other veteran who loves this country. No one bothered to call me and just ask me.

I have never, nor would I tolerate anyone expressing hateful racist views, espousing white supremist views or encouraging violence against our government. I have a well-known reputation of despising this type of hate. And it infuriates me that my own government has fallen into the false narratives sown by the Russians, Chinese and Iranians. Our government is spending valuable law enforcement and intelligence resources targeting patriotic American citizens whom they know are loyal to our country absolutely to their core.

I believe, this is the most effective counterintelligence operation ever conducted against the U.S. by our enemies. And that is what it is. This is an offensive counterintelligence operation perpetrated by our enemies to divide us against ourselves.

The CSIS brief makes this interesting suggestion in their report, "It would be worth examining whether the deployment of soldiers to controversial battlefields such as Iraq and Afghanistan triggered a backlash against U.S. society and the government (much like with the Vietnam War); whether military personnel have been increasingly influenced by the political polarization prevalent in the United States; or whether military personnel have been more active on the internet and social media platforms, which has contributed to radicalization. In addition, there may be other social, economic, educational, or cultural variables at play, along with the possible proliferation of charismatic individuals that have spread propaganda in the military." [35]

It would seem to me that maybe we should look for larger influences in our current circumstances than looking at veterans, active duty, reservists, off duty and serving police officers who have sworn oaths to defend the constitution.

Maybe they are feeling the same way I am that our country is under attack and our constitution is being shredded right before our eyes. For those of us sworn to defend the constitution, our oaths never expire. This is not rhetoric. We believe this. So, enemies of our country, constitution and our liberty should expect us not to sit by and watch it happen.

In its concluding remarks the CSIS brief relates that, "Of broader concern, the U.S. government does not release data on terrorist attacks and plots, nor on the characteristics of perpetrators. However, if a centralized data collection effort were established, data analysis could offer an objective mechanism for apportioning counterterrorism resources and efforts relative to actual threats." [36]

What a concept. Transparency.

Senior Collection Strategist for Domestic Terrorism

When I got to NCTC to serve as the Senior Collection Strategist, I discovered my office was mostly run by former or joint assignment FBI employees. They apparently did not know about EO 12333 or seem to understand or care about the limitations on intelligence collection against Americans by the constitution. Nor had they read the following...

In September 2020, the "National Counterterrorism Center, together with FBI and DHS, held a conference to examine the U.S. Government's approach to confronting the threat of domestic terrorism (DT) and to inform future DT policy. The conference convened stakeholders from academia, the private sector, and across the Federal Government, including intelligence and Non-Title 50 agencies." [37]

Here were the key takeaways from the conference (*bolding added for emphasis*):

- Although the threat from **DT is not new**, radicalization and communication of DT actors has evolved in recent years and remains potent.
- Because an increasingly **larger part of the activity related to DT occurs online and is constitutionally protected, increased collaboration among partners—including academia, NGOs, and state, local, and federal law enforcement**—will help combat this evolving threat.
- Most conference participants agreed that **current federal criminal statutes do not include a distinct law criminalizing acts of DT, leaving prosecutors to rely on existing criminal statutes** to address DT-related offenses, **indicating a need for legislative review**.
- Most conference participants agreed that a domestic terrorist organization designation, similar to **the current process for designating foreign terrorist organizations, could be useful in combating DT**; however, DT actors in the Homeland and abroad are aware of the activities that merit designation and adjust accordingly to avoid prosecution.
- Noting the **legal challenges to enacting a domestic terrorist organization designation**, there was support for using the foreign terrorist designation process to proscribe DT analogues overseas. (Legal challenges called the constitution. Was there really support?)
- Legal mechanisms available to some foreign partners, e.g., to ban DT groups, are **at odds with U.S. civil liberties**. Creating a DT designation in the United States could be **perceived as government overreach and/or unconstitutional**.
- Conference participants noted the significance of the role of terminology in DT, as definitions laid out in statute are used to determine the allocation of tools and resources to departments and agencies. Using **terminology solely derived from authorities can be**

restrictive, proscribing which departments/agencies participate in DT efforts, and lacks the flexibility to be useful for all U.S. Government DT efforts. This impacts how the U.S. Government responds to DT threats, requiring changes in existing practices among the interagency.

o There is **no whole-of-government DT threat picture**, largely because the U.S. Government does not have a common terminology to describe the threat. The absence of a common understanding of how threat departments/agencies prioritize DT issues differently results in a lack of analytic research and production on DT threats, and in turn reinforces the lack of policymaker prioritization. [38]

This was one of the first documents I read when I arrived at NCTC in October 2020. It was only a month old, but the office leadership had participated in the conference. It was their conference. While others in the office claimed to have read it, they conveniently disregarded most of the limiting factors such as agency authorities or that pesky thing called a constitution.

- **FBI Domestic Intelligence Activities**

There were other issues my government bosses seemed unfamiliar with, the ProPublica article points out: "The reasons (for no federal domestic terrorism statute) date to 1975, when an inquiry by the Church Committee of the U.S. Senate documented that the FBI had abused its powers by engaging in a pattern of spying on American citizens in groups ranging from the Black Panthers to the Ku Klux Klan. The government placed strict limits on the ability of the FBI and other agencies to infiltrate and track such organizations, with new laws and rules establishing more rigorous requirements for surveillance on Americans than foreigners. Today, FBI counterterrorism officials make a point of saying they target individuals rather than groups, and violent acts rather than ideologies." [39]

The program was called, "COINTELPRO. The FBI began COINTELPRO—short for Counterintelligence Program—in 1956 to disrupt the activities of the Communist Party of the United States. In the 1960s, it was expanded to include a number of other domestic groups, such as the Ku Klux Klan, the Socialist Workers Party, and the Black Panther Party. All COINTELPRO operations were ended in 1971. Although limited in scope (about two-tenths of one percent of the FBI's workload over a 15-year period), COINTELPRO was later rightfully criticized by Congress and the American people for abridging first amendment rights and for other reasons." [40]

We need to know what percentage of the current workload of the FBI is dominated by domestic extremism as opposed to other threats like China and cyber.

I believe there are striking similarities between the activities carried out against candidate Donald Trump and his supporters to the activities conducted by the FBI against Martin Luther King. [41]

So, none of this is new. The FBI pattern of exceeding their authorities is well documented and as such the FBI has been specifically limited in its authority to carry out these activities by the government in the past.

To be clear, I, unlike many who have lost all faith in the FBI, believe the FBI means well but they are too willing to skirt the law and, in fact, cross the line regarding domestic intelligence activities.

This is what I believe happened regarding the counterintelligence investigation into candidate Trump and his campaign. The FBI leadership assumed Hillary Clinton would win in 2016 so no one would ever find out about the forged emails (redacted) or the falsified FISA warrants. The FBI did these things because they never thought anyone would find out.

Why does the FBI seem to disregard the law when it suits them? I am not someone who thinks it is a cabal of evil Satan worshippers or some other nonsense conspiracy. I think it is nothing more than bureaucratic inertia or political cronyism (what President Trump calls the "Deep State").

Its unethical leadership for sure. It is an abuse of our trust. It is a violation of their oath to protect the constitution. It is abuse of power. Mostly, it is simply the belief that they will not get caught and that they know better than we do what the constitution says.

In their minds, they are the FBI, and they investigate Americans, therefore, they think they are above the law. They think their poo does not stink. They think it is ok to do something they know is illegal so long as they do not get caught, or so long as the American people do not find out exactly how willing the FBI is to disregard the constitution to "get their man."

- **The Intelligence Community**

Members of the intelligence community, except for the FBI (they are a law enforcement organization that does some intelligence stuff) know intelligence is about strategic advantage and indications and warning to <u>prevent</u> threats to our country.

The FBI does not prioritize preventing threats, they prioritize arrests and prosecutions. These two things are at crossed purposes when it comes to intelligence operations, and I have several personal examples from over the years.

(redacted)

(redacted)

This is a difference between intelligence collection and criminal investigations. Intelligence officers collect intelligence to prevent future threats. The FBI wants evidence to prosecute. The FBI did not care (redacted) in the future, they only wanted a prosecution.

Why this is important is because the intelligence community has information about all these types of activities before and after the individual arrives. The FBI does not have the cultural expertise, the technical knowledge nor the training to conduct these types of intelligence debriefings. And they do not prioritize them.

(redacted)

(redacted)

This is again because they put prosecutions in front of preventing a threat.

(redacted)

- Attorney General's Investigative Guidelines (Redacted) Special Report September 2005

The FBI has a history of problems running confidential human sources with regard to their domestic intelligence collection operations. According to The Federal Bureau of Investigation's Compliance with the Attorney General's Investigative Guidelines (Redacted) Special Report from September 2005 Office of the Inspector General: "Phillip B. Heymann, the former Deputy Attorney General and Assistant Attorney General in charge of the Criminal Division, observed: [S]ome informants are responsible citizens who report suspected criminal activities without any hope of return. In the middle, other informants live in the midst of the criminal underworld and inform largely for cash. Still others, at the other pole, are charged with serious crimes and cooperate with law enforcement officials in return for the hope or promise of leniency."[42]

The agencies which focus primarily on intelligence collection know money is the least effective form of control over a source and coercion (promises of leniency) are not tolerated. That is why what the FBI did to Gen. Michael Flynn is so horrendous. The FBI threatened to go after General Flynn's family if he did not plead guilty to a crime he did not commit. That is called coercion. This fundamental difference in conducting intelligence operations or criminal investigations as the FBI calls them, is why the FBI continues to be viewed by some as not being trustworthy or ethical when it comes to intelligence operations.

Throughout the Domestic Terrorism Conference Report from September 2020, it was identified that the various agencies were limited by their authorities. "The authorities panel included academic and civil liberties experts who discussed whether current DT authorities should be expanded, how, and against whom; the merits of applying terrorism designations in the domestic realm; and lessons that can be drawn from historical and foreign-partner case studies."[43]

Key takeaways from the conference included: "Federal statutes designate many terrorism-related activities as criminal, but membership in groups with violent or extremist ideologies is protected until espousing violence crosses a threshold of intending to incite—or inciting—such violence. From a law enforcement perspective, a criminal DT statute could provide additional authority to open investigations, bolster information sharing, and may aid in securing DT resources; and finally, from the civil rights community's perspective, existing authorities sufficiently address DT; DT is a policy problem that requires better alignment of resources to the threat, not a law problem; most NGO representatives that attended the conference did not support designation."[44]

So, to be clear. Having an ideology that is hateful or even despicable or deplorable is protected under the constitution. But, according to law enforcement participants during the conference "a criminal DT statute could provide additional authority to open investigations, bolster information sharing, and may aid in securing DT resources." Basically, what they were saying is,

"We know that the constitution protects this activity called free speech, but we want a DT statute anyway."

How about this suggested solution during the conference: "Explore creating a DT criminal statute and/or designating DT organizations <u>for deterrence purposes</u> and provide additional federal violation to authorize predication of an investigation." [45]

So, basically, the FBI wants to create a domestic terrorism statute to deter free speech and other constitutionally protected activities. You read that correctly. They want to "tamp down on hate speech" just as I had been saying throughout my U.S. Senate campaign. Hate speech is another term for free speech.

Curiously, the Domestic Terrorism Conference identified the following as something that would "derail" U.S. efforts against domestic terrorism. The report stated, "Our criteria for publicly labeling attacks as DT is opaque and inconsistent." [46]

Further demonstrating how little the FBI and others understand or care about the fact that domestic terrorism is not an ideological problem. The reason supposed domestic terrorism attacks are difficult to stop is because they are lone actors who are most often suffering from mental illness and that pesky constitution that stands in their way of labeling them terrorists.

When it came to domestic terrorism operations FBI and DHS provided two interesting takeaways. One that "Speech activities protected under the First Amendment of the constitution should be viewed as a factor, not a constraint." [47] And that "Panelists noted that federal law enforcement's goal is to prosecute actors, rather than groups, that commit violations of federal criminal law." [48]

What this means is, according to the FBI, the constitution should NOT be viewed as a limit on their power, just as something they needed to mitigate or circumvent.

My favorite part of the entire September 2020 Domestic Terrorism Conference Report are some of the suggested solutions.

- Explore creating a DT criminal statute and/or designating DT organizations for deterrence purposes and provide additional federal violation to authorize predication of an investigation. [49]

Interpreted to mean "We really just want a DT statute to tamp down on hate speech (or speech we don't like). We need it so we can get around the 1st Amendment."

- Create a cohesive and coordinated U.S. Government effort to publish, engage, and communicate among ourselves, with the private sector, and to the public. [50]

What? This sounds like a need for more transparency. Imagine a whole-of-government approach to talking about domestic terrorism. What a concept? They were doing just that in the September 2020 Domestic Terrorism Conference and ignoring the suggestions and many of the identified limitations.

- Establish a clearer picture of what the U.S. Government does and needs that is easier for civil society, NGO, and private sector partners to understand. [51]

This sounds like a need for more transparency. Essentially, the FBI is saying civil society, NGOs, and our private sector partners such as academics do not understand domestic terrorism. They are the FBI, and they understand domestic terrorism.

I think these organization understand exactly what the FBI wants to do, and they do not agree it is a domestic terrorism problem. This is not a problem with the constitution, it is a problem with mental health. It is a problem with the FBI thinking they can stop people from thinking what they want to think or worse create laws to intimidate people and silence them or target them for their free speech.

The continued conversation regarding domestic terrorism is not about stopping domestic terrorism attacks, it is about silencing people. It is about thought crime. Some politicians, believe or rather want us to believe it should be a crime to have a different opinion than they have. That is why racists and white supremacists are considered "domestic terrorists," but ANTIFA rioters who burn cities are "champions for justice." This is not about domestic terrorism; it is about "thought crime."

- **Known Problems with the FBI Criminal Informant Program**

Ultimately, the FBI wants more authority to investigate Americans who might be planning violence. Their current authorities already allow them to recruit sources within extremist organization through financial renumeration and judicial coercion.

The 2005 IG Review found: "The most serious compliance problems in the FBI's Criminal Informant Program, particularly with respect to the Guidelines' provisions requiring periodic suitability evaluations of confidential informants; the timely communication of instructions to informants; and the authority of confidential informants to engage in otherwise illegal activity." [52]

The IG review also points out: "We believe the principal reasons for these compliance problems were inadequate administrative and technological support; the FBI's failure to hold first-line supervisors and case agents accountable for guidelines violations; burdensome collateral duties assigned to many Confidential Informant Coordinators; and inadequate training for case agents, Supervisory Special Agents, Informant Coordinators, and Division Counsel. Particularly with regard to the Criminal Informant Program, the Guidelines violations we found were troubling and merit immediate attention." [53]

The 2005 IG report also noted, "With respect to the conduct of preliminary inquiries, however, we found a notable failure to adhere to the requirement to document in a timely fashion the extension or closure of preliminary inquiries, or the conversion of a preliminary inquiry to a full investigation." [54]

This is evidence of the FBI repeatedly bending or just ignoring the rules they themselves created to legally, ethically and morally carry out these activities. They don't seem to hold themselves to account according to this report.

What the FBI was asking for was more authority to investigate people who are exercising their 1st Amendment constitutionally protected rights. They know what they want, but they don't care. They want a domestic terrorism federal statute so they can "legally" violate American's civil liberties.

With all this in mind, should we entrust the FBI with more authorities to investigate "domestic extremists?"

As a very poignant case in point, BuzzFeed News recently released analysis on the Michigan governor case (BuzzFeed News, WATCHING THE WATCHMEN, by Ken Bensinger and Jessica Garrison), which seems too substantiate that the FBI will do whatever it takes to get their man, even paying veterans to spy on their fellow citizens and financially facilitate and encourage and enable the radicalization of American's who are already suffering from mental health issues in my opinion or are intensely frustrated with the state of our country. [55]

UPDATE: 2019 OIG Review of the FBI CHS Validation Process

To all my fellow HUMINT professionals out there reading this. This next section is critical to understand and every lawyer who defends a client against the FBI and their confidential sources this is a must read. The FBIs Confidential Human Source (CHS) Program is NOT a professionally run activity by the most basic standards across the intelligence community. This is not an Agent problem. This is an absolute organizational failure. [56]

I say this as someone who has been part of U.S. Human Intelligence (HUMINT) operations for over 15 years. I have served as a professional HUMINT collector, senior intelligence analyst, senior HUMINT targeting officer, senior HUMINT operations officer and as a senior collection strategist. If there is any doubt about my collected highlights of their failures to operate professionally you should read the Office of the Inspector General's November 2019 Audit of the Federal Bureau of Investigation's Management of its Confidential Human Source Validation Processes from which this information is derived. [57]

According to this report, "The AG Guidelines also require validation activities at various intervals, including initial and annual CHS validations, and enhanced validations for certain special categories of CHSs, such as long-term CHSs." [58]

And "In addition to the AG Guidelines, the U.S. Intelligence Community provides CHS validation guidance through its National HUMINT Manager Directive 001.08, which establishes a common set of validation standards for collectors of intelligence." [59]

In this audit the OIG provides sixteen (16) recommendations to help the FBI better manage its CHS program but for me it is unconscionable that the supposed intelligence activities being conducted against American citizens by the FBI is so wrote with these critical failures to conduct even the most basic intelligence processes. [60] Even the most junior US Army intelligence collector would have run away from these operations and likely reported them to a higher headquarters.

- **FBI Source Validation Process**

The AG Guidelines and the FBI's Validation Manual require that all special category CHSs, such as long-term CHSs, receive an enhanced review every 5 years however, the FBI simply ignores this requirement or implemented ad-hoc changes periodically to essentially ensure that long-term CHSs never received these reviews. [61]

The FBI has a policy regarding the validation (ensuring that the human source providing information to the FBI is providing truthful information and does not have other personal factors which make the person inappropriate for these activities - drug use, criminal activities, vulnerabilities to outside influences etc.). However, the FBI literally ignored every facet of its own policy especially regarding its most important sources considered "long term." [62]

According to the report, the FBI knows that - "This process, known as validation, is a fundamental responsibility of intelligence collectors, including the FBI. Validation serves as an essential component of FBI human intelligence (HUMINT) because it assists in ensuring that information obtained from any CHS is accurate, authentic, reliable, and free from undisclosed influence." [63]

If you don't do validation, you are not doing HUMINT. Not only did the FBI ignore their own regulations the FBI never trained any of the individuals responsible for the validation process, left the oversight committees understaffed or just didn't bother to have any headquarters oversight at all. The audit states that these failures "increased risk" to these operations. In actually, the FBI seems to have deliberately sabotaged the validation process knowingly putting at risk (risks posed by overly familiar and non-objective handling agent and CHS relationships, and poor operational security) the safety of the CHS's as well as their own agents. [64]

The FBI maintains no comprehensive roster of its CHS pool nor keeps track of what CHSs were aligned against for purposes of reporting. There were no policies for the methods of communicating with these sources to protect either the source or the agent or the operation. [65]

The FBI changed its validation procedures multiple times without following their own policies and procedures regarding these changes. The FBIs database for CHS operations is reported to be essentially useless for simple activities like knowing how long a source has been run by the FBI. [66]

According to the FBI's Policy Guide, the continued handling of a long-term CHS by the same handling agent for 5 consecutive years, and every 5 consecutive years thereafter, requires SAC approval. In addition, this approval may not be delegated, and the Special Agent in Charge (SAC) may only approve continued handling by the same handing agent for "good cause." [67]

The FBI's Policy Guide definition of 'good cause' included the following justifications:

(1) whether the handling agent has a unique role in an investigation supported by the CHS, to the extent that the investigation may face impediments due to reassignment of the handling agent; (2) whether

reassignment of the handling agent would diminish the FBI's ability to obtain information in a reliable manner due to the sophisticated or technical nature of the CHS reporting and the knowledge base of the handling agent; or (3) whether there are other circumstances that affect the effective operation of the CHS, including the availability of other handling agents with the requisite experience or capability to operate the CHS. [68]

However, without any oversight or an effective validation process or even a first line supervisor with adequate training there is no way to identify any of the above problems.

The OIG audit determined that the FBI did not ensure that all handling agents requested and received SAC approval for the continued handling of CHSs more than 5 years and could not provide adequate data to make an evaluation. "The FBI could not provide us with a universe of requests for approval for continued CHS handling." [69]

So, in brief the FBI does not even know how many long term CHSs it has and very likely almost none of them have ever had an adequate validation review.

- **Inadequate Validation Personnel and Training**

According to the report, "At the field offices, the Assistant Director in Charge or Special Agent in Charge (SAC) is responsible for ensuring a local CHS program that contributes to the FBI's collective CHS base. To assist in fulfilling this responsibility, Special Agents in the field offices ("handling agents") recruit, vet, handle, and communicate with CHSs. [70] In addition, supervisors oversee handling agents and are responsible for the completion of quarterly CHS reporting. FBI Assistant Special Agents in Charge (ASAC) are responsible for reviewing and submitting annual CHS reports, that serve as the field office's review of the CHS file - a responsibility that cannot be delegated." [71] However, none of these personnel receive training in the validation process and claimed repeatedly to the auditors that they did not know how important validation was.

FBI leadership has significantly reduced the number of intelligence analysts conducting validations. According to the report, in February 2010, the FBI had 213 FBI headquarters personnel dedicated to validation efforts. As of March 2019, FBI headquarters had only a single validation unit comprised of 29 personnel - an 86 percent decrease in FBI headquarters validation personnel since February 2010. [72] According to the report, the FBI Assistant Director for the Resource Planning Office stated, "that in anticipation of the 2013 sequestration spending cuts, the FBI identified certain FBI headquarters resources to be cut, including a portion of DI's Intelligence Analysts." The same official explained to the auditors that, "when sequestration did not come to pass as expected, the resources were not restored and were instead re-allocated to the field offices." [73]

The HUMINT Services Unit II responsible for validations did not have a cadre of trained intelligence analysts to perform long-term validations. According to the report, "Actual intelligence analysts typically receive 13 weeks of formal training, including multiple weeks of analytical writing courses" but the Agents in charge of overseeing CHS were given only on the job training and were then responsible for seeing to the training of their own replacements. [74]

According to the report "The Department and the FBI did not comply with Human Source Review Committee composition requirements. The OIG reviewed "16 meetings conducted between February 2016 and November 2018 and found that for each HSRC meeting: (1) the FBI had only one of the two required FBI OGC attorneys; (2) the Department did not have a DAAG present from the Criminal Division for any of the meetings; (3) the number of additional federal prosecuting office attorneys participating in the meetings varied between one and three; and (4) there was no attorney designated by the AAG for National Security." [75]

And that typically, "two HSRC members-one Department official and one FBI official-generally decided all HSRC long-term CHS continued use requests." [76]

FBI and Department officials told the auditors, "that that HSRC composition for the period we reviewed has left a few individuals assuming a large burden of risk and that, with the exception of the one Department official who shared in the decision-making burden, the other Department officials generally did not actively participate." [77]

Some Departments were supposedly not even aware that they were expected to participate in the review process.

- **Operational Activities – Source Reporting and Communications**

Safely communicating and properly documenting and protecting the operational reporting (meetings with the sources) are supposedly critical aspects of the FBI's intelligence gathering process. However, according to the OIG report the databases containing this information is of little use in managing sources much less the validation process. [78]

According to the OIG report, "Secure communications are vital to the operational security of FBI investigations across all FBI programs. Failure to use secure communications can allow for the interception and exploitation of highly sensitive information by adversaries and potentially compromise the safety of FBI personnel as well as CHSs. Although the FBI's Policy Guide discourages agents from using email, text message, facsimile, and other electronic communications when communicating with CHSs, it does not prohibit them. Further, the policy does not positively identify the types of devices, applications, and methods that should be used when communicating with CHSs to mitigate operational and safety risks." [79]

"The disparity in type of device used appeared to be based on a number of factors, including: (1) the handling agent's field office, (2) the handling agent's operational division, (3) the handling agent's supervisor, (4) the ease of obtaining non-FBI-issued devices within the field office, and (5) the experience of the handling agent." [80]

"Nearly (REDACTED) of the survey's respondents stated that they had never received formal training on communicating with CHSs or that the training they had received was inadequate." [81]

How is it that "the FBI lacks clear and concise guidance on communicating with CHSs." [82]

How is this possible? Because they are not a professional intelligence organization.

The sensitivity and security of communicating with human sources is a critical activity as is the documentation of all intelligence reported and meeting activities. Mistakes are not tolerated in the IC. It is because of this, I believe the FBI are not a professional intelligence organization.

Not surprisingly the audit report noted, "Because of the importance and sensitivity of many of the FBI's law enforcement, national security, and intelligence operations, as well as the risks to both FBI personnel and CHSs, we recommend that the FBI develop and implement a policy that clearly informs FBI personnel of the acceptable platforms for communicating with CHSs and provides training to its workforce on the policy." [83]

Recommend? Really?

If this was any organization other than the FBI all operations would be halted immediately.

- Why is it so bad? – Legal Discovery

According to the report, "the FBI Validation Manual states that the FBI has an abiding interest in establishing the validity of each CHS." [84]

Accordingly, "the FBI has a duty to ensure that each CHS is reporting truthfully and to document those instances of red flags, derogatory reporting, and anomalies." [85]

However, the auditors were told by multiple Intelligence Analysts that "they received guidance to only state the facts and not to conduct analysis, report conclusions, and make recommendations." [86] Multiple FBI officials told the OIG audit personnel that they believe "field offices do not want negative information documented in a CHS file due to criminal discovery concerns and concerns about the CHS's ability to testify. Because some U.S. Attorney's offices will not use a CHS at trial if there is negative documentation in the CHS's file." [87]

Apparently not all U.S. Attorneys have these concerns.

So, the reviewers are being told specifically not to make assessments or recommendations because it will make the source unusable for purposes of prosecutions.

I discuss this exact same behavior regarding FBI agents not reporting mental health warning signs of their suspects during investigations for fear they would not be able to prosecute them.

For all intents and purposes the FBI is deliberately excluding information they know will inhibit their ability to prosecute someone because it will be discoverable in a legal case.

The professional answer to this issue is as a CHS Coordinator emphasized to the auditors, "the historical value of documenting issues with the CHS because handling agents change, and new handling agents can only know the risks if they are documented." [88]

So, if problems are not documented then the source is handed off to subsequent handlers without a true understanding of the risks associated with the source.

According to the OIG audit, and I agree completely "By withholding potentially critical information from validation reports, the FBI runs the risks that (1) prosecutors may not have complete and reliable information when a CHS serves as a witness and, thus, may (May have? May have?) have difficulties complying with their discovery obligations; and (2) future handling agents may be deprived of relevant information about the CHS that could not only jeopardize an investigation but also put the agent's safety and potentially sensitive information at risk." [89]

The fact is, by not providing this incredibly important information regarding the validation review, the prosecutor is prevented from meeting the discovery responsibilities.

In Brady v. Maryland, 373 U.S. 83 (1963), the US Supreme Court held that prosecutors are required to notify defendants and their attorneys of any favorable evidence: held – "Suppression by the prosecution of evidence favorable to an accused who has requested it violates due process where the evidence is material either to guilt or to punishment, irrespective of the good faith or bad faith of the prosecution."[90]

I wonder if there are any emails from attorneys instructing analysts to exclude specific information from validation reviews.

- **The Blame Game**

The FBI has known about these issues and have done little to correct their problems. The 2019 audit report noted that the FBI Inspection Division conducted a National Program Review in 2013 regarding the AG Guidelines. It reported, "that existing CHS policies were disjointed, inadequate, and out of date." [91]

And that "The 2013 National Program Review also reported that the DI's interactions with the IPO were not productive. IPO employees reported that a lack of engagement by the DI was a constant source of frustration and constituted "the single biggest policy risk to the FBI" at the time." [92]

People inside the FBI are telling their own reviewers that the process is a mess, and it is "the single biggest policy risk to the FBI." [93]

To cover their rear ends, "Some FBI officials attributed this (lack of proper validation) to the FBI not adequately communicating the importance of the annual report in the FBI's CHS validation process." [94]

As I said, even the most junior collector in the actual intelligence community that deals with HUMINT knows the validation process of a source's veracity and an unbiased understanding of the sources vulnerabilities is paramount to effective operations.

According to the audit, "the 2013 National Program Review found that field offices did not understand the annual CHS report's role or importance in the CHS validation process and reported that nearly 43 percent of the 2,101 agents who responded to the survey indicated the annual report was not effective in identifying CHS risks." [95]

The validation process is not useful in identifying risks because the process deliberately prevents the reporting of red flags, derogatory information, anomalies, analysis, conclusions, and recommendations. All the information needed to make a informed decision.

In 2013 the Inspection Division "recommended that the DI disseminate guidance to the field offices highlighting the annual CHS report as a fundamental component of validation and develop a training module illustrating how it can mitigate risk."[96] However, in 2019, the FBI could not provide the auditors with "any evidence that this internal recommendation had been implemented."[97]

These are the facts:

- Between FY 2012 and FY 2018 the FBI spent an average of $42 million annually in payments to its CHSs.
- As of May 2019, nearly 20 percent of the FBI's CHS base met its definition of a long-term CHS (more than 5-years).
- FBI validation personnel were specifically discouraged from documenting their conclusions and recommendations.
- The number of personnel tasked with conducting long-term CHS validations was insufficient considering the size of the long-term CHS validation backlog.
- Validation personnel at every level lacked adequate training to evaluate the veracity of reporting or the handling of the sources.
- The joint DOJ and FBI Human Source Review Committee (HSRC) (responsible for the validation review process) consistently fell short of the composition requirements of the AG Guidelines.
- The FBI lacks an automated process to identify, track, and monitor long-term CHSs to know when a CHS requires special review.
- The FBI lacks an automated process to document approvals that allow the same agent to continue to manage a CHS more than five years.
- Between 2011 and 2019, the Directorate of Intelligence (DI) implemented different validation processes without incorporating them into policy, missing the opportunity to go through the formal deconfliction process that should have identified its non-compliance with AG Guidelines requirements for long-term CHSs.
- As of November 2019, the most recent iteration of the validation process, developed in 2017, had still not been incorporated as official policy.
- The importance of the annual CHS report in the overall validation process has supposedly not adequately communicated to FBI field offices.
- The FBI lacked clear guidance to inform its personnel of the acceptable platforms for methods of communicating with CHSs.
- Internally, the FBI is not ensuring its highly classified CHS reporting platform is safeguarded from unauthorized access, increasing the potential for insider threat risks.
- The FBI has no process for making sure CHSs are aligned with its highest threat priorities.
- There is essentially no independent headquarters oversight to ensure CHS risk is effectively mitigated.
- The databases which hold CHS data, is known to have significant data quality issues.
- FBI Directorate of Intelligence (DI) management on its own decided to implement a new review system which did not comply with the AG Guidelines.
- The FBI used electronic communications to communicate to field offices regarding changes to the CHS validation process causing confusion and noncompliance.
- The FBI never approved an updated Validation Manual, supposedly because of continual leadership turnover within the DI.
- The FBI could not account for the full scope of a CHS's use, regardless of

whether the CHS had operated for 5 years, 10 years, or longer.
- CHS production reviews, which analyze a CHS's contributions to investigations, did not include the corroboration of information as a component of the production (the term used for intelligence information provided) review.
- The FBI discouraged validation personnel from making any overall conclusions or recommendations based on the information gathered.
- The absence of conclusions or recommendations deprived HSRC members of sufficient information to make decisions regarding the continued use of CHSs.
- The deliberate limiting of CHS review recommendations and conclusions prevents prosecutors from meeting their legal discovery responsibilities.
- The FBI maintains no way to reliably identified long-term CHSs; notify the appropriate unit that a validation was due; or track long-term CHSs to ensure a validation was completed.
- The FBI was unable to provide the auditors with an accurate list of how many CHS validations were in backlog.
- The FBI was unable to provide any evidence that field office personnel received guidance on their roles and responsibilities in the validation process.
- The Assistant Division Counsel who had received no training on the validation review process was advised not to sign off on the panel results because of all the problems with the validation process.
- Due to the immense backlog of validations "it is not feasible to conduct reviews of all annual CHS reports because of the limited number of validation personnel."
- These failures on the part of the FBI leadership increased its risk of missing warning signs, especially for questionable CHSs. [98]

Conclusion - The FBI is not an intelligence organization. They are a law enforcement organization that pretends to do intelligence.

It's not domestic terrorism problem. It's a mental health problem.

The FBI knows that in virtually every instance of "targeted violence" (mass shooter or bombing), that the individual was someone suffering from mental health and or psychological problems. That does not mean a person who is planning something terrible should not be stopped. What it means is we should be prioritizing mental health rather than intelligence activities directed against American citizens. All the signs are there. What is missing is the appropriate response and necessary resources.

I was in a conversation with one of my co-workers at NCTC who had spent years working this issue in the FBI and she told me that (redacted)

(redacted)

This is horrific. If this is true, then FBI agents conducting investigations are deliberately falsifying investigative records by excluding important information which could lead to a person getting help instead of a pair of handcuffs or prison. Not just domestic terrorism cases but all cases. It also likely makes it easier to violate a person's civil liberties more easily if they conveniently leave out mental health indicators.

I am sure the FBI would say: Their agents are not trained in assessing a person's mental health. If there is even a suspicion that a person being investigated poses a danger to himself or others because of their mental health, the FBI should be required to bring in a healthcare professional to provide expert analysis of the information not cover up the persons mental health issues so they can continue to spy on them and ultimately try to prosecute them.

- Lack of Imagination - Black Swans

Very soon after I started the job as a Senior Collection Strategist on Domestic Terrorism, I sat in a meeting led by my government boss. The meeting was with the Domestic Terrorism team from FBI via video teleconference.

By this point, I had read all the important documents from the conference, several National Security Council memos on domestic terrorism as well as virtually all the most current domestic terrorism reporting and finished intelligence.

I had also read and begun drafting the two documents which were my responsibility at NCTC – (redacted) Not to mention that I had been a counterterrorism expert for several years. That is why they picked me for this job.

Remember, I had been reading this material for years so there was not much in the classified holdings at that point I had not already read. In the past, I had not had a need-to-know specifically for some of the domestic terrorism/extremism information contained in FBI holdings which is almost 98% Unclassified / Law Enforcement Sensitive (LES).

Understanding what the FBI had in its holdings was important once I was in this position. Over the course of a few weeks, I had read virtually everything the FBI had published on domestic extremism over the last several years. You may be surprised but there was not much

I already had concerns because the very first thing the FBI suggested in (redacted) was that (redacted)

Understandably, I could not believe what I was reading because even the September 2020 Conference had identified this as a virtually impossible bar to cross and those in the FBI should have known about their troubled history regarding domestic intelligence operations against U.S. citizens for ideological purposes such as Communist leanings, racism or membership in the Klu Klux Klan as well as their troubling history regarding running confidential informants more broadly.

Very interestingly, during that first meeting, on the video teleconference, I asked the FBI at the other end of the teleconference, had they done any "red teaming." Red teaming is essentially writing up what potential domestic terrorism events might look like and developing strategies to mitigate them. Or had they conducted any analysis on unlikely "black swan" events regarding domestic terrorism? A black swan event is an event which could not be anticipated because no one would ever even consider it.

You know what I mean – like a kid in Kenosha, Wisconsin getting attacked with Molotov cocktails and having to defend himself with an AR-15 from ANTIFA, or maybe a rally in DC getting subverted by agitators creating a crisis which results in them taking advantage of the crowd's passion to storm the Capital Building. These would be considered black swans.

It became immediately clear that none of these senior FBI Domestic Terrorism "experts" had any clue whatsoever about what I was talking about. (redacted)

I reiterated, that I was not talking about (redacted) and told them what I meant by red teaming or black swan events. They said that they had not.

These are common terms across the intelligence community, but it was clear that no one in the room including my boss had any idea what I was talking about. All I was asking was if anyone had given any thought to likely and even unlikely events that could kick off something bad. No one was even able to answer the question. I was stunned.

Loss of Faith and Trust in Government

The FBI's case against General Flynn is known now to have been completely contrived, like the counterintelligence investigation into the Donald Trump campaign during his 2016 campaign. Both events were perpetrated against American citizens for solely political purposes. The bureaucrats did not like Trump or Flynn, and they never thought Trump would win so no one would ever know what they did.

Some members of the DoD and CIA leadership did not like General Flynn because he had spoken out against Obama's plan to leave Iraq which ultimately resulted in the birth of ISIS and the lies to the American people about winning against ISIS in Iraq.

Ultimately this event, our departure from Iraq under then President Obama, I believe is the greatest political military blunder in our history and caused the deaths of hundreds of thousands of Syrians, Iraqi, Afghani, Pakistani, and Yemeni people. This actually caused the massive upheaval in the Middle East known as ISIS. Our military withdrawal also allowed the Russians and the Chinese to expand globally, particularly into the Middle East.

The CIA did not like Flynn because he also pushed for the Defense Intelligence Agency to have its own clandestine service which the CIA hated.

But the main reason they had to get rid of General Flynn I believe as the National Security Director for President Trump was because he would have discovered the illegal counterintelligence investigation carried out by the FBI against candidate Trump. These things have all now been revealed.

Was anyone fired at the FBI? Nope. FISA warrants were falsified. Classified emails regarding (redacted) altered. Illegal and unconstitutional activities carried out by the FBI. Anyone fired? Nope.

I knew the very day Donald Trump said he was being spied upon that he probably was being spied upon and it would have to be a counterintelligence investigation. I suspected this at the time because of all his global foreign business contacts. I knew this because this is what we do.

It is important we (the U.S. government) do these kinds of investigations because there are people, foreign spies, out there who will recruit Americans to run for political office or get jobs in government to gain access to intelligence information or influence our government. We regularly conduct these types of investigations and I support them under normal circumstances.

With regard to President Trump, Carter Paige and Michael Flynn however, once it became clear there was nothing there, they should have immediately stopped, and they did not. Instead, they falsified intelligence information to violate these Americans civil liberties and carry out illegal intelligence operations against U.S. citizens.

So, yes, I knew that Donald Trump probably was being "investigated" and it would have to be a counterintelligence investigation.

But it is critical to understand that in order to carry out this activity it could not be a criminal investigation. A counterintelligence investigation can only be conducted by the FBI against an American citizen if there is reason to believe that the person may be under the influence of a foreign government.

Very few of these counterintelligence investigations ever go to trial or result in a prosecution. **(redacted)**

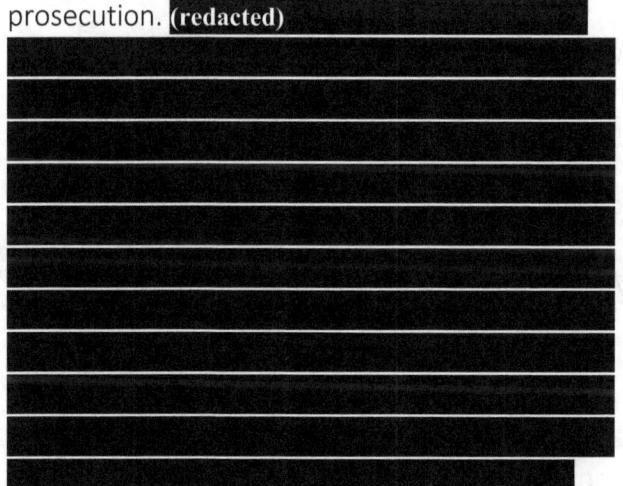

But then Trump won in 2016. Flynn would have figured it out, so they had to get rid of Flynn and fast.

- **The Domestic Terrorism Prevention Act of 2017**

On March 2, 2021, FBI Director Christopher Wray testified before the Senate Judiciary Committee on the January 6th attack on the U.S. Capitol. During his opening statement Committee Chair Dick Durbin (D-IL) showed a heart wrenching video of the Capital Police officers and what they went through during the January 6th, 2021, event. This should never have happened. But, not for the reasons and the excuses many claim it was Donald Trump's fault. As I said, those with me were stunned that it was happening.[99]

Sen. Durban said that this it isn't new. "They might as well have worn white robes."[100] Basically, he was calling everyone who was in DC on January 6th to support the President a white supremacist.

Sen. Durban called everyone who supported the President insurrectionists and all of them white supremacists.

He never once makes clear in any way who he is limiting these comments to. He then restates what Director Wray has stated many times over the last few months. "Violent white supremacists are the most persistent and lethal threat in the homeland. And pose a growing terrorist menace."[101]

Sen. Durban goes on to point out that he had drafted a Domestic Terrorism Prevention Act as early as 2017, which makes the claim that "white supremacy and far-right extremism are among the greatest domestic-security threats facing the United States. Regrettably, over the past 25 years, law enforcement, at both the Federal and State levels, has been slow to respond. Killings committed by individuals and groups associated with far-right extremist groups have risen significantly."[102]

In the 2019 Domestic Terrorism Prevention Act of 2019 it states that "[s]ince September 12, 2001, the number of fatalities caused by domestic violent extremists has ranged from 1 to 49 in a given year." The report noted: "[F]atalities resulting from attacks by far-right wing violent extremists have exceeded those caused by radical Islamist violent extremists in 10 of the 15 years and were the same in 3 of the years since September 12, 2001. Of the 85 violent extremist incidents that resulted in death since September 12, 2001, far right-wing violent extremist groups were responsible for 62 (73 percent) while radical Islamist violent extremists were responsible for 23 (27 percent)."[103]

The Act lists the following as justification for the need of such an Act. Fatal terrorist attacks by far-right-wing extremists include—

(A) the August 5, 2012, mass shooting at a Sikh gurdwara in Oak Creek, Wisconsin, in which a White supremacist shot and killed 6 members of the gurdwara;

(B) the April 13, 2014, mass shooting at a Jewish community center and a Jewish assisted living facility in Overland Park, Kansas, in which a neo-Nazi shot and killed 3 civilians, including a 14-year-old teenager;

(C) the June 8, 2014, ambush in Las Vegas, Nevada, in which 2 supporters of the far-right-wing "patriot" movement shot and killed 2 police officers and a civilian;

(D) "the June 17, 2015, mass shooting at the Emanuel AME Church in Charleston, South Carolina, in which a White supremacist shot and killed 9 members of the church;

(E) the November 27, 2015, mass shooting at a Planned Parenthood clinic in Colorado Springs, Colorado, in which an anti-abortion extremist shot and killed a police officer and 2 civilians;

(F) the March 20, 2017, murder of an African-American man in New York City, allegedly committed by a White supremacist who reportedly traveled to New York "for the purpose of killing black men";

(G) the May 26, 2017, attack in Portland, Oregon, in which a White supremacist allegedly murdered 2 men and injured a third after the men defended 2 young women whom the individual had targeted with anti-Muslim hate speech;

(H) the August 12, 2017, attack in Charlottesville, Virginia, in which a White supremacist killed one and injured nineteen after driving his car through a crowd of individuals protesting a neo-Nazi rally, and of which former Attorney General Jeff Sessions said, "It does meet the definition of domestic terrorism in our statute.";

(I) the July 2018 murder of an African-American woman from Kansas City, Missouri, allegedly committed by a White supremacist who reportedly bragged about being a member of the Ku Klux Klan;

(J) the October 24, 2018, shooting in Jeffersontown, Kentucky, in which a White man allegedly murdered 2 African Americans at a grocery store after first attempting to enter a church with a predominantly African-American congregation during a service; and

(K) the October 27, 2018, mass shooting at the Tree of Life Synagogue in Pittsburgh, Pennsylvania, in which a White nationalist allegedly shot and killed 11 members of the congregation.[104]

All told this is eleven violent extremists killing forty Americans over the course of nine years. I hate it that there was even one. But, somehow this does not seem to rise to the level of an existential threat to America. It just doesn't. This sounds to me like eleven assholes.

The Act further articulates for some unknown reason the horrific attack on Muslims in New Zealand and six in Canada as somehow more evidence we have a domestic terrorism threat in the US. [105]

Then as more justification to increase the federal government's ability to stop domestic terrorism the Act mentions that there was one Coast

Guard Lieutenant that was a racist and advocated for "focused violence."[106]

The Act does not require the federal government to do much. It requires the FBI report include information regarding infiltration of the uniformed services and law enforcement in federal, state and local government by white supremist, neo-Nazis, an analysis of domestic terrorism in the United States going back to 1995 by category (REMVE, HVE, militia and anti-government, I suppose anti-abortion and environmental as well), the number of initiated domestic terrorism related preliminary investigations and the final assessments of each, the number of full investigations, number of arrests, the number of indictments, prosecutions, and convictions as well as weapons recovered etc.[107] Sounds like something we would already have right? Why don't we?

The FBI would also be expected to share intelligence to address domestic terrorism activities; conduct an annual, intelligence-based assessment of domestic terrorism activities in their jurisdictions; and formulate and execute a plan to address and combat domestic terrorism activities in their jurisdictions.[108] Shouldn't they already be doing these things? Twenty-one Democrat and one Independent Senator were sponsors for the bill. Not one Republican. Why not?

During the hearing Sen. Chuck Grassley (R-Iowa) said something that I think few in the Halls of our government believe. He said, "We must examine all forms of extremism. A narrow view of these matters would not be intellectually honest. Such Attacks on police officers etc. (referring to the politically motivated attacks on police officers across the country). Extremism is both from the left and the right." And further points out the hypocrisy when actual left-wing violence is tolerated and even promoted but right-wing "extremism" (not even violence) is considered a crime warranting laws prohibiting it.[109]

Basically, only the right is willing to say all violence and hate is bad. The left promotes and encourages their violence as being fully justified.

The problem is tolerance of leftist violence is what is causing the right-wing "extremism." They must understand this. We can only assume it is deliberate.

During this hearing, Senator Grassley reminds us that it was a violent leftist madman who is the only person thus far to attempt a mass political assassination of a group of unarmed Republicans playing baseball. No mention from the left regarding this assassination attempt by one of their adherents.[110]

- **FBI sowing fear. Making matters worse.**

According to Director Wray in his prepared comments "The January 6th attack, was domestic terrorism."[111] That the January 6th event was conducted for the specific purpose of terrorizing the American people to bring about a political change. If that were the case, then why did everyone just leave?

According to Director Wray, domestic terrorism is metastasizing and not going away any time soon. It is a top concern for the FBI. And in June 2019 he elevated RMVE to our highest threat priority alongside ISIS and HVE. He stated that the FBI will not tolerate agitators and extremists that plan or commit violence. And that goes for violent extremists of any stripe.[112]

He offers another list of threats such as the Solar Winds intrusion, huge range of other cyber threats, nation states and criminal organizations and toxic combinations of the two. As well as the vast unrelenting counterintelligence threat from China and the alarming threats of violence toward law enforcement.[113]

He goes on to say there was no threat assessment from the FBI leading up to the January 6th rally. When asked "What the FBI knew and when they knew it and why didn't it rise to the level of an assessment."[114] His answer is not surprising to me, but it is probably to anyone who thinks that there is a nation-wide threat from domestic terrorism.

According to the Director one report from the internet, out of the Norfolk Field Office and almost immediately emailed and published in law enforcement channels specifically the DC PD and the Metro PD. The Situational Information Report (SIR) was raw, unverified, and uncorroborated information posted online. This report was quickly disseminated (within an hour) in three different ways – emailed to the Joint Terrorism Task Force, passed verbally in the command post briefing, which included Capital Police and MPS, and third posted on a law enforcement portal as raw, unverified, and uncorroborated. He states himself that he did not see the brief until several days after the 6th and that the handling of the report was consistent with normal processes.[115]

Director Wray does also point out that there were quite a number of militia violent extremists such as Proud Boys and Oath Keepers as well as other REMVE also but that there is no evidence at this time of fake Trump protesters.[116]

According to The George Washington University Program on Extremism report from March 2021, *"This is Our House!" A Preliminary Assessment of the Capitol Hill Siege Participants* researchers, stated that of the almost 300 people arrested for their actions on January 6th, they "were able to identify 33 individuals with military backgrounds. These included 31 veterans, 1 current member of the National Guard, and 1 current member of the Army Reserves. 36% of individuals with military backgrounds also had concrete ties to various extremist organizations, including the Proud Boys (7), Oath Keepers (4), and Three Percenters (1)."[117]

So out of the almost 300 arrested only twelve appear to be involved in militias. Does this sound like an attack or an insurrection?

Additionally, GWU reported that "Based on preliminary information, this report evaluates three main categories of individuals who stormed the Capitol: militant networks, organized clusters, and inspired believers."

Militant networks are characterized by hierarchical organization and chains of command and accounted for thirty-three (33) of the arrests. Organized clusters are described as being composed of small, close-knit groups of individuals who allegedly participated in the siege (political bias revealed) together, usually comprising family members, friends, and acquaintances and accounted for eighty-two of the arrests. Inspired believers were reportedly individuals, were neither participants in an established violent extremist group nor connected to any of the other individuals who are alleged to have stormed the Capitol and accounted for the majority of the arrests, one-hundred and forty-two.

When asked what number of the individuals were arrested (about 270 by FBI and about 30 more from local and state authorities[118]), what percentage of them were REMVE or white supremacy affiliated individuals? What other ideologies - HVE, international etc. How many jihadists, white supremists, and left-wing anarchists?

The Director makes clear that many were militia extremists, a few anti-government and racially motivated extremists <u>but most would not fall into any type of extremist category</u>.[119]

According to GWU report at the time of its writing, "257 individuals have been charged in federal courts for their involvement." According to their research, individuals arrested are as young as 18 and as old as 70. 221 are men and 36 are women. They came to the Capitol from 40 states, and 91% traveled from outside the Washington, DC metropolitan area. 33 individuals had known military backgrounds.[120]

When confronted regarding resources and how these resources are aligned, the Director admits that the bulk of the FBI's domestic terrorism resources are targeted at RMVE and militia extremists but does not know how much is aligned to other types of extremists, in particular ANTIFA.[121]

I believe he probably knows the answer to this because after having been the Senior Collection Strategist for Domestic Terrorism at NCTC, even I know the answer to this. (redacted)

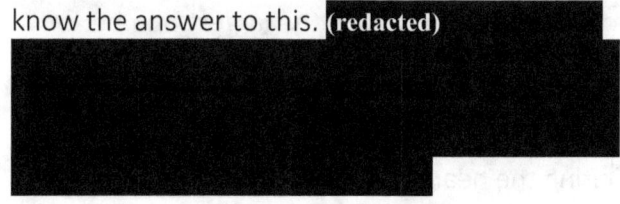

- How is the FBI going to save us?

When asked what was needed to improve the collection of intelligence on extremists, he stated that they needed to develop more and better sources within these groups (hire more Americans to spy on their fellow Americans), better understand and overcoming the supposed tradecraft being used by these individuals (as if these people were professional spies using tradecraft). But ultimately, he said the more arrests the FBI makes, the more they will learn about the "threat," and their tactics and strategies.[122]

So, according to the Director of the FBI, the FBIs plan to defeat domestic extremist ideology from all facets is to recruit more Americans to spy on other Americans (He does not mention the use of judicial extorsion.) and arrest more Americans to learn more about the threat.

I think that is the very reason people do not trust the FBI to begin with.

To his credit, Director Wray states that the FBI are not investigating people based on their ideological views, they are only concerned about violence. He has stated specifically people can believe whatever they want no matter how horrific it might be, they simply cannot plan to or carry out violence. The problem lies in the efforts he is supporting to circumvent the constitution in order "to protect us."

Wray says, "Something that is very important to us at the FBI. We focus on the violence and the violations of federal law. The ideology comes into it as a further piece of the puzzle as we build out the case. Our focus is on the violence. We don't care what ideology motivates somebody."[123]

Sen. Lindsey Graham (R-SC) asked Director Wray, "Do you have enough people and resources to deal with all the threats we have been talking about this morning."[124]

To which the Director answers that "Everywhere he goes people tell him he should be doing more. But not very many asking them to do less." Then he goes on to say "We need more agents. We need more analysts. We need more data analytics."[125]

Sen. Graham asks very specifically whether the Proud Boys, Oath Keepers Antifa or the KKK are domestic terrorist groups? When he is told there is no list, the Senator asks, "What does it take to make the list?"[126]

Wray's reply, "Well, there is as you may know Senator, under federal law, U.S. law there is no list of domestic terrorism organizations the same way there is for foreign terrorist organizations."[127]

Graham says, "So why don't we think about how to gather better information and expose some of these groups. If they were on a list, would it make it easier for you?"[128] This report I hope helps to answer that question.

Again, the Director says, "I think the issue of whether or not to designate or have a formal mechanism for designating domestic terror "groups" in the same way we do Al-Qaida or ISIS. I think there is reasonable debate about whether or not it would really advance legal..."[129]

Ultimately, the Senator states, "I don't know if we should have one (a domestic terrorism federal statute) or not, but I think it's time to think about it."[130]

Hopefully, this report will help answer that question.

- **The Looming Threat of Global White Supremacy**

During the hearing and clearly not having any understanding of the conversation thus far, Sen. Dianne Feinstein asks the Director, "Why is the threat of white supremacy terrorism so prevalent in this country?"[131] As if we have white supremacy attacks every day in the U.S.

The Director answers artfully, "Some of that is a sociological question that I am not sure I am really the right person to address. Certainly, as you say it has been the biggest chunk of our RMVE cases and itself the biggest chunk of our domestic terrorism case load overall. And the most lethality over the last decade has been from these same extremists."[132]

But then he goes on to talk about the true difficulty regarding this issue we are facing. He states that, "The things that drive these people, I think range. One of the things we struggle with in particular is, more and more, the ideologies, if you will, that are motivating these violent extremists are less and less coherent. Less and less linear. Less and less easy to pin down. In some cases, it seems like people are coming up with their own sort of customized belief system. A little bit of this. A little bit of that and they put it together. Maybe they combine that with a personal grievance of something that has happened in their lives. And that drives them. So, trying to get our arms around that is a real challenge."[133]

This is exactly why I am writing this report. The problem is not a domestic terrorism problem, Wray is talking about it being a mental health problem without saying specifically because he knows it will cost the FBI funding.

Sen. Dianne Feinstein also articulates during this hearing how there has been a massive increase in gun sales but makes no connection at all the nationwide violence from BLM and Antifa.[134] What she really does not understand is that today we probably have the largest number of Americans who have literally no personal relationship with firearms and little training.

During the hearing, Sen. Cornyn (R – TX) calls out the FBI's lack of anticipating this event on January 6th as a "failure of imagination."[135] That is why in the military we think about black swans as I have discussed.

He also notes that there is no domestic terrorism charge and instead people are charged with assaulting federal officers, tampering with documents or proceedings, unlawful entry, disorderly conduct, conspiracy, theft of government property. Sen. Cornyn asks Wray, "Do you think the current laws are adequate?"[136]

Wray's response, "Certainly, you would be hard pressed to find any FBI Director who wouldn't welcome more tools in the toolbox."[137]

This is his way of saying that he wants a domestic terrorism federal statute to circumvent the 1st Amendment. He appears here to have realized that this isn't going to go over very well or possibly that he has been advised by lawyers that a domestic terrorism federal statute isn't something they should be asking for because it will not stand up in the Supreme Court because well, there is that pesky constitution to consider.

During his questioning Sen Cornyn makes a statement followed by a question which is very important. "It's the FBIs responsibility to deal with counterintelligence investigations. Correct? These include active measures..."[138] (Measures used by our adversaries to sow chaos in the U.S. such as happened in 2016.) "Is it true that our foreign adversaries used the events of January 6th, as a field day? With an intent to discredit the United States and its institutions?"[139]

Wray responds, "Foreign adversaries, a number of them, are leveraging the events of January 6th to amplify their own narratives to try to push out propaganda, misinformation, to try to in their view accelerate what they think of as United States decline."[140]

As I have said, this is the single most effective counterintelligence operation ever perpetrated against the American people and the FBI Director just said it himself. The problem is he is part of the operation. Unwittingly, our own government is helping to discredit its own government in the eyes of the world by continuing to promote the idea that we have a domestic terrorism threat which we do not.

UPDATE: 2021 Data on Hate Crimes in America

According to recent reporting by the FBI there were "7,759 criminal incidents and 10,532 related offenses as being motivated by bias toward race, ethnicity, ancestry, religion, sexual orientation, disability, gender, and gender identity."[141]

"There were 7,554 single-bias incidents involving 10,528 victims. A percent distribution of victims by bias type shows that 61.9% of victims were targeted because of the offenders' race/ethnicity/ancestry bias, 20.5% were victimized because of the offenders' sexual-orientation bias, 13.4% were targeted because of the offenders' religious bias, 2.5% were targeted because of the offenders' gender identity bias, 1% were victimized because of the offenders' disability bias, and 0.7% were victimized because of the offenders' gender bias." Additionally, "There were 205 multiple-bias hate crime incidents that involved 333 victims."[142]

The FBI reported that across the U.S., a country with 330 million people, there were "7,426 hate crime offenses classified as crimes against persons in 2020, 53.4% were for intimidation (3965), 27.6% were for simple assault (2049), and 18.1% were for aggravated assault (1349). Twenty-two (22) murders (0.003%) and 19 rapes (0.003%) were reported as hate crimes."[143]

No demographic information was provided regarding the perpetrators of the murders or rapes. I think this information would be valuable in understanding exactly how racist the U.S. is. You would think that with such a small data pool, just 41 cases of rape and murder, they would want to report who the racists were. So, Americans would know who to look out for.

The FBI also reported that, "Of the 6,431 known offenders, 55.2% were White and 20.2% were Black or African American. Other races accounted for the remaining known offenders: 1.1% were Asian, 1.1% were American Indian or Alaska Native, 0.5% were Native Hawaiian or Other Pacific Islander, and 5.6% were of a group of multiple races. The race was unknown for 16.4%."[144]

Why was the race unknown in 16.4% of the instances? How do we know if it was an actual hate crime?

Could it have been an instance of someone pretending to carry out a hate crime or claiming that it was a hate crime? Stranger things have happened.

Likewise, how valuable is it to know that there were approximately 64 Asian offenders? Who were they hateful towards? This is just not very valuable data.

That there were 3550 hate crimes perpetrated by white people is valuable information because that means out of 330 million Americans, we for sure have 3550 racists. Proving we don't actually have a racism problem in the U.S. If we did, I would expect this number to be higher than 3550 white people who hate assumedly non-white people.

- **What the FBI really thinks about the Congress**

If you want proof of what the FBI really believes about the politicians and who they answer to, just watch when Sen. Whitehouse points out during this hearing that seven out of nine Senate hearings the Senate committee has not received answers to questions they sent to the FBI.[145]

Basically, the FBI just flips the Congress the bird and tells them screw off. This is what I mean by the fact that the bureaucracy does not think they, the FBI, are accountable to our elected representatives, the congress.

Sen. Mike Lee (R-Utah) confronts Director Wray regarding the FBI using geolocation data and asks how he is doing it. Is it being done through the FISA court or with probable cause warrants to collect this information from telecommunications companies?[146]

Wray pretends that he doesn't know the answer to these questions. This is another one of those instances where the FBI does things in the belief that they will not get caught violating people's constitutional rights.

Sen. Josh Hawley goes after getting these answers again and the Director again lies about what he knows. He likely could have said, "It would have to be discussed in a classified setting," but at no time does he say that. This is because he knows there are unconstitutional activities being conducted. In all likelihood, he believes the information will not be used in any legal case but it will be used to identify those people of interest so the FBI can then come up with other reasons they were brought to the FBI's attention. When asked about banks providing information to the FBI regarding the January 6th events, he again lies about not knowing if this is happening.

On the issue of violence generally, some Senators are starting to see the truth of things, that the domestic terrorism threat is not even close to the homicidal violence in the seventeen major inner-city neighborhoods plagued by violence.

Sen. Tom Cotton (R-Ark) brings up the violent international criminal organization plaguing the United States called MS-13. Unfortunately, he fails to ask if MS-13 poses a greater threat to the United States than the threat of white supremacists.[147]

Sen. Jon Ossoff (D-Georgia) enquires about the incredible crime wave gripping the United States particularly in the top 17 inner city neighborhoods.[148]

Wray claims there is no single factor driving the crime wave. He admits that these things don't get the headlines that other events do but makes no substantive comments on this pretending not to know the answer. If he doesn't really know the answer to this then we really do have a problem because they don't care at all what is happening in the cities that account for 8000 to 10000 violent homicides every year and ten times that number in attempted homicides.

- **Threats to the Homeland Over Time (2020 to 2021)**

During his statement before the House Homeland Security Committee, on September 17, 2020, on Worldwide Threats to the Homeland, Director Wray listed the threats arrayed against the United States, he listed domestic terrorist first, foreign motivated terrorists second, election security third, citizens access to encryption forth (imagine the American people having privacy in their private conversations), China fifth, and cyber sixth. This is done intentionally because the FBI needs to increase fear in order to justify expanding their authorities and budget.

The funny thing is the last four threats listed are priorities of other organizations. China and cyber are not FBI priorities they are DoD, CIA, NSA, NRO priorities. Certainly, they have a play in it when it comes to FBI domestic authorities, but they have virtually no play at all with China or cyber on scale.

In March 2021, he provides another list (a lot can change in six months): the Solar Winds intrusion, a huge range of other cyber threats, nation states and criminal organizations and toxic combinations of the two. "As well as the vast unrelenting counterintelligence threat from China and the alarming threats of violence toward law enforcement."[149]

As far as real threats go - there is only one in this list – China. China has its hands in all these threat streams, and they have a huge military, massive and very capable cyber army, and a massive economic engine to promote their influence around the world. Domestic terrorism and foreign terror threats are not and never have been a top tier threat to America in the homeland regardless of what people may have been led to believe. Never. They are certainly high profile and usually very emotional affairs, but China is the real threat we face today.

If that is true, I guess we should be asking how much of the FBI's resources are being directed at white supremist and right-wing extremists as opposed to "the vast unrelenting counterintelligence threat from China?"

What is the classification Law Enforcement Sensitive?

There is a public face of the FBI which covers up their mistakes and exaggerates threats regarding domestic terrorism. Then a private face (98% unclassified open-source information hidden behind LES classifications markings) which is much more accurate about what the FBI knows and assesses regarding these threats but the American people, especially our elected officials, are kept in the dark. This is done deliberately.

If you want proof, during the March 2nd Senate hearing Director Wray is asked, if the FBI could provide the memo regarding the threat report (the Norfolk SIR report) to the Senate. The Director of the FBI stated that this report was "Law Enforcement Sensitive." And as such, he would "see if we can make that available."[150]

This report is LES. It is unclassified information. He had just said the FBI had given it already to the DCPD, MPD and made it available on a nationwide portal for law enforcement. This is the FBI pretending LES is a security classification.

In the four months I was at NCTC I read virtually every finished intelligence report regarding all categories of domestic terrorism. I promise you less than 2% were actually classified (Secret or Top Secret) information. The other 98% is completely unclassified, yet it is deliberately kept from the American people and our elected officials by putting the LES handling caveat on their reports.

The definition of LES is unclassified. (U) LAW ENFORCEMENT INFORMATION NOTICE: This product contains Law Enforcement Sensitive (LES) information. No portion of the LES information should be released to the media, the public, or over non-secure Internet servers. Release of this information could adversely affect or jeopardize investigative activities. [151]

Another definition for LES is: LAW ENFORCEMENT SENSITIVE (LES) information is unclassified information originated by agencies with law enforcement missions that may be used in criminal prosecution and requires protection against unauthorized disclosure to protect sources and methods, investigative activity, evidence, or the integrity of pretrial investigative reports. Any law enforcement agency employee or contractor in the course of performing assigned duties may designate information as LES if authorized to do so pursuant to department specific policy and directives. [152]

(U) LES is a content indicator and handling caveat that indicates the information so marked was compiled for law enforcement purposes and contains operational law enforcement information or information which would reveal sensitive investigative techniques. LES information may be released or disclosed to foreign persons, organizations, or governments with prior approval of the originating agency and in accordance with all applicable DNI foreign sharing agreements and directives. [153]

I am not suggesting that LES information regarding ongoing investigations be available to the public but once it is no longer needed to facilitate a prosecution or investigation it should be.

I contend the FBI uses the handling cavate Law Enforcement Sensitive (LES) to deliberately get around legal restrictions regarding the classification of government materials. According to government regulations, there are prohibitions to the use of classification markings.

- o The only lawful reason to classify information is to protect national security.
- o Information must be declassified as soon as it no longer qualifies for classification.
- o Information must not be classified, continue to be maintained as classified, or fail to be declassified for any other reason.
- o Information is prohibited from being classified to conceal violations of law, inefficiency, or administrative error, to prevent embarrassment to a person, organization, or agency.
- o Or to restrain competition, or to prevent or delay the release of information that does not require protection in the interests of national security. In addition, basic scientific research and its results cannot be classified unless that information is clearly related to national security. [154]

There is no release date for LES material because it is not classified. The FBI treats LES as a classification despite it not being related to national security. I believe this is done to avoid unwanted scrutiny as well as "conceal violations of law, inefficiency, or administrative error, to prevent embarrassment to a person, organization, or agency." [155]

All LES means technically is "don't leave it laying around." But, by labeling it LES they could keep these documents out of the hands of the public and our political leaders indefinitely.

The funny thing is almost all these FBI reports on domestic terrorism marked LES were derived from open-source reports already available on the internet or derived from academic reporting.

I believe FBI reports are being marked LES so FBI analysts produce something, anything, when they should be producing these documents publicly so that the American people would have insight into what the FBI was thinking about domestic terrorism.

In way of a perfect example of what I am talking about - in 2009 a DHS Assessment was "leaked." The document was classified UNCLASSIFIED//FOUO (For Official Use Only). Which means its distribution should be limited only to those who have an official use for the information. Again, this is not a classified document. Nothing in it is classified. FOUO is used the same way LES is used, it is called a handling caveat. Basically, it means "don't leave this laying around." But it does not, I repeat does not, contain classified information. [156]

(redacted)

(redacted)

(redacted)

How was it expected to "influence domestic public opinion" or be "conducted in an overt and transparent manner" if it was NOT made public? Absolutely nothing in the product was in any way classified. So why limit distribution?

The answer is DHS and FBI do not really want people to know what they are thinking. They want to pretend to be transparent but not actually be transparent. This bureaucratic behavior is what gives rise to the antigovernment sentiment today. [157]

What was it they did not want the American people to know? The answer to that is that the assessment contained LES information. The overall classification was FOUO, but a small number of paragraphs contained LES information. [158]

Here is a breakdown of the information DHS and the FBI did not want the American people to know what they were assessing. These were the Key Findings of their assessment. (Underlining and bold provided to highlight the key points of their assessment of this extreme threat to America.)

(redacted)

(redacted)

(redacted)

(redacted)

(redacted)

(redacted)

(redacted)

(redacted)

(redacted)

Does this sound like something that went through any actual analysis with any rigor at all?

I could have made this assessment very easily.

Many Americans who believe in the U.S. Constitution will not take kindly to threats to the constitution. It also says that people who believe in the constitutional right to bear arms, in the constitution and who have served the country in the military pose a threat to America and are probably racists.

According to DHS and the FBI (redacted)
(redacted)
(redacted) According to the assessment of the DHS and the FBI here were the supposed causes of the increase in domestic extremism.

(redacted)
(redacted)
(redacted)
(redacted)
(redacted)
(redacted)
(redacted)

(redacted)

It would be very enlightening for the American people to know that the (redacted)
(redacted) The American people should know this. By publishing this information openly, the politicians would be stripped of their ability to craft the false narratives of threats looming around every corner in America. That is why the FBI does not reveal what they know and keeps their assessments behind fake classification markings like FOUO and LES.

- **Why mislead the American people?**

Money. The problem is, when they make public statements, they must make it seem like every threat is an existential threat to justify their continued growth of budget and expansion of "authorities."

If there really is no threat, they cannot justify an increase in resources. All bureaucracies do this not just the FBI. I have said for longer than I can remember government agencies are not mission focused they are budget focused. Their mission must keep expanding for their budgets to keep expanding. If the mission was ever considered complete, then they would have to reduce their budgets. Since the foreign terrorist threat is diminishing, the FBI needs to create a new boogeyman to replace it or there will be budget cuts.

During his statement before the House Homeland Security Committee, on September 17, 2020, on Worldwide Threats to the Homeland, Christopher Wray then the Director of FBI said "I am proud of their dedication to our mission of protecting the American people and upholding the constitution. Hostile foreign actors, violent extremists, and opportunistic criminal elements have seized upon this environment. As a result, we are facing aggressive and sophisticated threats on many fronts. Whether it is terrorism now moving at the speed of social media, or the increasingly blended threat of cyber intrusions and state-sponsored economic espionage, or malign foreign influence and interference or active shooters and other violent criminals threatening our communities, or the scourge of opioid trafficking and abuse, or hate crimes, human trafficking, crimes against children—the list of threats we are worried about is not getting any shorter, and none of the threats on that list are getting any easier." [159]

Does anyone believe that these threats such as opioids and crimes against children rank in "sophistication" to the threats of Russia, China, or Iran? Or how about malign influence from these countries? Or "active shooters?" These are all key words and phrases chosen specifically to raise peoples emotions.

He says, "the list of threats we are worried about is not getting any shorter, and none of the threats on that list are getting any easier." [160]

This is language for "The sky is falling. Give us more authorities and more money so we can save you."

He goes on to say "Preventing terrorist attacks remains the FBI's top priority. However, the threat posed by terrorism—both international terrorism (IT) and domestic violent extremism—has evolved significantly since 9/11. The greatest threat we face in the homeland is that posed by lone actors radicalized online who look to attack soft targets with easily accessible weapons." [161]

Lone actors radicalized online? **(redacted)** but deliberately removed when they speak in public. Why?

Because they know it is not a domestic terrorism problem if the cause is mental health. They cannot expect to receive more money or authorities to violate the 1st Amendment if they mention the fact that the main cause is mental health issues suffered by the perpetrators. This is clear to anyone who reads the conclusions regarding these incidents, but the FBI cannot say we have a mental health problem if they have any hope of getting more, more, more. More money. More authorities.

Listen to this statement – "More deaths were caused by DVEs (domestic violent extremists) than international terrorists in recent years. In fact, 2019 was the deadliest year for domestic extremist violence since the Oklahoma City bombing in 1995." [162]

That's interesting. What if the truth was that more deaths were caused by people suffering from mental health problems than international terrorists in recent years? Because that is the truer statement.

He is specific when he says - "The top threat we face from domestic violent extremists stems from those we identify as racially/ethnically motivated violent extremists (REMVE). REMVEs were the primary source of ideologically motivated lethal incidents and violence in 2018 and 2019 and have been considered the most lethal of all domestic extremists since 2001. Of note, the last three DVE attacks, however, were perpetrated by anti-government violent extremists." [163]

Could this be because the government is viewed as not being legitimate or ignoring the constitution when it suits them thus causing some American citizens to be reacting out of fear of government abuses of authority, disregard for the constitution or just willful disregard for the rule of law?

He goes on to say – "The FBI is involved only when responses cross from ideas and constitutionally protected protests to violence." [164] This is an important statement and one that everyone should hear. It means that according to the FBI you can say whatever you want. Provided it does not involve violence. What it does not consider however is that there are many people in America who think what happened with President Trump, Michael Flynn, Waco Texas, Ruby Ridge etc. means that the FBI can no longer be trusted.

I do not believe the entire FBI is corrupt. Most people serving at the FBI are proud, constitution loving Americans and they are embarrassed by the activities of these political class bureaucrats. I know because I have spoken with many.

What I propose is, all too often the FBI leadership has been willing to break the law and disregard the constitution when they do not think they are going to get caught. The act of doing this makes the entire organization illegitimate in many American's eyes because the common everyday American believes if you swear an oath to uphold the constitution as your first act as a trusted agent of the federal government that should be paramount. Repeated "violations" are not mistakes, they are unwritten policy.

Unless something changes, between covering up their mistakes and exaggerating the threats of "domestic terrorists," they will only lose more and more of the trust and confidence of the American people.

2020 DHS Homeland Threat Assessment

In October 2020, DHS released its Homeland Threat Assessment. In it, it lists cyber, foreign influence activity, economic security, terrorism, transnational criminal organizations, illegal immigration, and natural disasters stating that this is the ""Whole-of-DHS" report on the threats to the Homeland." [165]

This is an excellent and comprehensive document if you really want to understand the true threats arrayed against us. It will be interesting to see how the assessed threat changes with the new administration.

The cyber threat is acute to say the least. The threat is against all levels of government, the military and the private sector from nation-state and non-nation state actors from "array of cyber-enabled threats designed to access sensitive information, steal money, and force ransom payments." Russia, China, and Iran pose the most capable cyber actors, but they are joined by cyber criminals. The entire range of cyber threats is articulated including the threats posed to our democratic processes. [166]

The foreign influence threat is also acute. Foreign governments are amazingly effective in "amplifying the U.S. socio-political divide" across the whole of the U.S. from the local level to the federal level. Primarily carried out by Russia, and a close second by the Chinese, disinformation campaigns are directed at the legitimacy of our elections, census, and our nations COVID-19 response. The sky is the limit when it comes to foreign disinformation. These efforts are targeted directly against vulnerable populations and intended to exacerbate the division so that the U.S. will tear itself apart from within. Are they winning? I believe China and Russia are winning because we are fighting among ourselves. [167]

The economic threat to U.S. economic security is tied mostly to the COVID-19 pandemic but hits on topics such as the exploitation of U.S. academic research, Chinese foreign investment, threats to the U.S. supply chain, and violations of trade law and policies by our economic rivals. [168]

Transnational organized crime is covered in the report – Mexico-based cartels, illicit drugs, human smuggling, exploitation of others for profit (think sex trafficking and child exploitation etc). [169]

Illegal immigration is covered as a threat to the U.S. in the report. It is difficult to believe that the current administration will see this as a threat. But the Trump Administration report sets a baseline for post Trump. [170]

Natural disasters are included in the report as a threat but only peripherally. [171]

The terrorist threats to the Homeland section of the report is what we are concerned with here. The report leads off with "Ideologically motivated lone offenders and small groups pose the most likely terrorist threat to the Homeland, with Domestic Violent Extremists presenting the most persistent and lethal threat." [172]

The report states, "The domestic situation surrounding the COVID-19 pandemic creates an environment that could accelerate some individuals' mobilization to targeted violence or radicalization to terrorism. Social distancing may lead to social isolation, which is associated with depression, increased anxiety, and social alienation." [173] In all my research on domestic terrorism from government sources this is the first-time mental health is mentioned as a potential motivator to violence and it isn't even a very strong statement.

Also, of note, the report points out the concerns many have regarding violent extremist media and social media which exacerbates the fears of the public regarding topics such as COVID-19, the 2020 election, the burning of cities, attacks on police and ideologically aligned violent protests etc. The report covers at a remarkably high level all the myriad threats to the homeland and lumps them all into terrorism in the homeland – white supremist, anti-government, anti-authority, as well as the potential threat posed by conspiracy and "political commentary some might view as controversial." [174]

The report mentions the continued threat of foreign terrorist organizations (FTOs), including al-Qaida and the Islamic State of Iraq and ash-Sham (ISIS) as well as Iran and Lebanese Hizballah. It even mentions the "The overall global weapons of mass destruction (WMD), and the "risk of intentional chemical, biological, radiological or nuclear incidents in the homeland and abroad has likely increased." [175] This is truly one of the best general consumption documents I have seen regarding the myriad of threats we face today.

Except for the few instances I have mentioned above, I have not read or heard any mention of the mental health crisis or the inner-city violence plaguing 17 "neighborhoods" (Not entire cities. The violence is very localized.)

In the U.S. suicide accounts for 40,000+ deaths each year, not to mention the 1.4 million attempted suicides. Homicides in 17 neighborhoods in the U.S. account for 8,000+, not the mention that there are over 10 times that number in attempted homicides which due to inner-city gang violence. Opioid deaths account for 70,000+ deaths each year, many of which are believed to be suicides.

Five.

Five domestic terrorism deaths in 2020. But no mention of the tens of thousands of deaths caused by these known threats. Nor the fact that they are related. Why?

The Mental Health Problem

It is my contention that if we instead focused on the mental health crisis in the U.S., we would have a profound effect on an actual number of people and reduce homicides, suicides, and mass shooter events. We know we cannot stop every mass shooter or violent individual who wants to make a bomb, but we certainly could put a dent in the opioid's crisis, the mental health crisis, the inner-city gang violence, and homicide crisis.

Also, no mention by the government at all regarding the loss of trust of many Americans with the U.S. government, fueled by covered up mistakes and foreign influence operations which serve to divide us. No mention of any government responsibility in the loss of in trust with the American people.

Instead, DHS recently created the Center for Prevention Programs and Partnerships (CP3) and have begun additional efforts to comprehensively combat domestic violent extremism. [176]

The stated purpose of CP3 is "to improve the Department's ability to combat terrorism and targeted violence, consistent with privacy protections, civil rights and civil liberties, and other applicable laws." This all sounds like a step in the right direction, except DHS Secretary Mayorkas deliberately obfuscates what the actual causes are when he says. "Individuals who may be radicalizing, or have radicalized, to violence typically exhibit behaviors that are recognizable to many but are best understood by those closest to them, such as friends, family, and classmates." [177] What he is saying is, it is not a domestic violence problem, it is a mental health problem.

The DHS press release states, "DHS's efforts are grounded in an approach to violence prevention that leverages behavioral threat assessment and management tools and addresses early-risk factors that can lead to radicalization to violence." [178]

Again, not being clear he is saying the problem is mostly a mental health issue. He cannot say this outright because DHS would not be able to use the boogeyman of domestic terrorism to ask for more money or expanded authorities. DHS also does not want to interfere in what the FBI wants which is also more authorities and more money.

On May 12, Secretary Mayorkas appeared before the U.S. Senate Appropriations Committee to testify on "Domestic Violent Extremism in America." [179]

In his prepared remarks he articulates exactly what I have been saying throughout this document. The threat of domestic terrorism is "complex, more dynamic, and more diversified." He states explicitly that racially or ethnically motivated violent extremists and anti-government or anti-authority violent extremists, specifically militia violent extremists are dangerous and will target "target law enforcement, government personnel, and government facilities." [180]

I agree that lone actors are often motivated to violence because of "false narratives, conspiracy theories, and extremist rhetoric" in social media and other online platforms. However, he again makes no mention whatsoever about the mental health of most of the perpetrators or the lack of government transparency which leads to many of these false narratives, conspiracy theories, and extremist rhetoric. He also makes no mention of the fact that because of some of the recent actions of the U.S. government such as the illegal FBI investigations and the threats and coercion applied against American citizens has damaged the faith of many Americans in the government.

- **The Purge**

This next part is terrifying to me, and it should be to all Americans. Secretary Mayorkas says DHS "is taking a new approach to addressing domestic violent extremism – both internally and externally." [181] What does he mean "internally?"

Here it is, "Among my top priorities is to ensure that our personnel can perform their critical missions, that they feel safe and secure at work, and that the fabric of our department is not penetrated by hate or violent extremism. In light of this commitment, I announced last month an internal review to address potential threats related to domestic violent extremism within DHS and ensure we are not compromised in our ability to protect our country." [182]

What he is saying is that employees of DHS who love the constitution (supposed anti-government, second amendment and militia extremists) pose a threat to the DHS from within.

This is McCarthyism pure and simple. I think we should be asking DHS to tell us explicitly what the criteria is for the "review?"

We need to know if other organizations in the government are purging their ranks of people who do not agree with their vision of America or the constitution?

January 6th Rally at the Capital

According to the Senate report, *Examining the U.S. Capitol Attack: A review of the security, planning, and response failures on January 6.* If you read just the executive summary you will be led to believe that it was a planned attack. "Rioters, attempting to disrupt the Joint Session of Congress, broke into the Capitol building, vandalized and stole property, and ransacked offices. They attacked members of law enforcement and threatened the safety and lives of our nation's elected leaders."[183]

And only "Due to the heroism of United States Capitol Police ("USCP") officers, along with their federal, state, and local law enforcement partners, the rioters failed to prevent Congress from fulfilling its constitutional duty." Is that what really happened? [184]

- Whose fault, was it?

According to the Senate report - "response failures of the entities directly responsible for Capitol security—USCP and the Capitol Police Board, which is comprised of the House and Senate Sergeants at Arms and the Architect of the Capitol as voting members, and the USCP Chief as a non-voting member—along with critical breakdowns involving several federal agencies, particularly the Federal Bureau of Investigation ("FBI"), Department of Homeland Security ("DHS"), and Department of Defense ("DoD")." And "The Committees' investigation uncovered a number of intelligence and security failures leading up to and on January 6 that allowed for the breach of the Capitol. These breakdowns ranged from federal intelligence agencies failing to warn of a potential for violence to a lack of planning and preparation by USCP and law enforcement leadership." [185]

According to the report, "Despite online calls for violence at the Capitol, neither the FBI nor DHS issued a threat assessment or intelligence bulletin warning law enforcement entities in the National Capital Region of the potential for violence. FBI and DHS officials stressed the difficulty in discerning constitutionally protected free speech versus actionable, credible threats of violence." [186]

"As a result, critical information regarding threats of violence was not shared with USCP's own officers and other law enforcement partners." [187]

"On January 5, an employee in a separate USCP intelligence-related component received information from the FBI's Norfolk Field Office regarding online discussions of violence directed at Congress, including that protestors were coming to Congress "prepared for war." This report, similar to other information received by IICD, was never distributed to IICD or USCP leadership before January 6." [188]

The report articulates all sorts of reasons for the breach of the Capitol such as, inner-agency communication processes, intelligence failures across the IC, failures to prepare plans for violence based on a single on-line report which was uncorroborated and unsubstantiated, the trucks with the police riot gear were locked, and the lack of proper protective equipment or training to hold off the tens of thousands (hundreds actually) of "attackers".[189]

Supposedly because the USCP couldn't provide a detailed map of the location of the USCP officers that somehow played a part in the failure. The report also makes known that the officers were not authorized to use available less-than-lethal munitions.

I don't think that "less lethal" munitions would have been the best course of action, but the Senate apparently feels that maybe the situation would have been better handled if they had used rubber bullets on their fellow American citizens. That's one way to go I suppose.

My favorite blame game they play is when the report states that "communications were chaotic, sporadic, and, according to many front-line officers, non-existent." [190]

Also, the reason for the "attack" was that there was no request for National Guard support based on the "threat" reporting found on the internet and worse did not know the proper method of requesting National Guard support. Finally, when a formal request was made to the Acting Secretary of the Defense, the DoD didn't respond fast enough. [191]

Basically, its everyone's fault except for theirs. Not one mention by the Senate report regarding the incredible tensions created in the country. Not one.

The Committees' Recommendations - "Based on the findings of the investigation, the Committees identified a number of recommendations to address the intelligence and security failures leading up to and on January 6. Recommendations specific to the Capitol Complex include empowering the USCP Chief to request assistance from the DCNG in emergency situations and passing legislation to clarify the statutes governing requests for assistance from executive agencies and departments in nonemergency situations. To address the preparedness of the USCP, the Committees recommend improvements to training, equipment, intelligence collection, and operational planning. The Committees further recommend intelligence agencies review and evaluate criteria for issuing and communicating intelligence assessments and the establishment

of standing "concept of operation" scenarios and contingency plans to improve DoD and DCNG response to civil disturbance and terrorism incidents. These scenarios and plans should detail what level of DoD or DCNG assistance may be required, what equipment would be needed for responding personnel, and the plan for command-and-control during the response." [192]

The report also claims that this was an intelligence failure. It's the ICs fault. Senators believe that the IC should, "Review and evaluate handling of open-source information, such as social media, containing threats of violence. Review and evaluate criteria for issuing and communicating intelligence assessments, bulletins, and other products to consumer agencies, such as USCP. Fully comply with statutory reporting requirements to Congress on domestic terrorism data, including on the threat level and the resources dedicated to countering the threat." [193] What do they think they were doing already?

Interestingly, according to the Senate Report, and as I suspected, the Capitol Police were the first to use "chemical munitions" on the crowd as they advanced on the Capitol building.

I am in no way condone any of the violence, but I do wonder as I have stated that if the Capitol Police had not done this, we may not have had this event at all. I have wondered if I had been at the front would I have tried to calm the passions of the crowd or been able to counteract the efforts of agitators.

The report makes clear that "After overrunning USCP's security perimeter on the West Front of the building, rioters pressed towards the Capitol building—climbing the inaugural platform and scaling walls. The only remaining security perimeter consisted of the USCP officers positioned around the grounds, who were overwhelmed and outnumbered. USCP officers attempted to hold back the rioters with chemical munitions, such as oleoresin capsicum ("OC") spray, more commonly known as "pepper spray." [194] And that is when all hell broke loose.

As a professional intelligence officer, I pride myself on being able to see through the optic of the other side of a situation. I cannot imagine what the police officers and our elected officials must have been thinking being on the other side of what must have seemed like a million angry Americans. They were outnumbered. They were surrounded. They were scared. They had a job to do. They were probably just as awestruck as we were watching this happening in our great country.

I have said it several times and I still believe it. We, the "right-wing," conservatives, we don't do this. In fact, I had just the day before stood down a crowd in front of the Supreme Court doing just that. This should never have happened.

I don't blame the USCP, or the National Guard, the FBI or any one of the other agencies that the Senate report blames. I blame the politicians for feeding the anxiety of the American people on both sides of the ideological spectrum. I blame the media who pretend to report the news but prey on people's fears for profit. The politicians on both sides do the same thing.

- **Domestic Terrorism of not?**

According to retired FBI agent Thomas O'Connor, in a ProPublica article the day after the rally, he had no doubts about what to call the activities on January 6th. "The definition of terrorism is the use of a threat of force or violence to influence the policy of a government." [195] He also said, "You had people who physically and violently broke down doors and stopped a legislative action. This is an act of domestic terrorism, in my opinion."[196] Neither of these statements is supported by facts. These are his opinions.

FBI declared in 2019 that there have been "more deaths caused by domestic terrorists than international terrorists in recent years." [197] This kind of statement is what I am talking about. Because I wonder how the supposed threat of "domestic terrorism" compares to the threats from Iran, China, Russia, the southern border, drug addiction, gang violence, drunk drivers, lightning strikes, tornados, constipation, heart disease, cancer, suicide etc.

I also wonder if we would even be talking about domestic terrorism if we just accepted that the constitution protects all free speech, even speech we do not like, and that law abiding citizens should not be worried about gun confiscation because owning firearms is an unalienable right.

We know most mass shooters are suffering from mental health issues, there is an increasing amount of distrust among the American people because of legitimate concerns about the threats to their liberty by the very government claiming to protect them, and finally we know they want to use intelligence capabilities to circumvent the 1st Amendment. Finally, there is no transparency when the FBI or any part of the U.S. government screws up only aggravating the distrust.

O'Connor believes that anyone who kills someone based on their race should be considered a terrorist. [198] This is again the wrong headedness I am talking about, calling someone a terrorist elevates them in the eyes of others rather than just calling them a murderer. It is this kind of thinking that has given legs to terrorists throughout history. In most cases, real terrorists use the media to achieve their goals and labelling hate as terrorism is going to increase even more of these crimes.

According to the ProPublica article, "Trump's repeated description of federal agencies as part of a so-called deep state has also hampered enforcement of domestic terror crimes, O'Connor and other former agents said. Some local law enforcement agencies have held back in assisting FBI-led counterterrorism task forces, the former senior FBI national security official said. In addition, the mutual affinity of the president and far-right groups has discouraged some federal officials from pursuing the threat as actively or prominently as they should, he said." [199]

This is ridiculous. The reason most organizations will not participate with the FBI is because what they want to do is either against the law, not within their authorities or because the FBI has a long track record of crossing the line.

Let us not forget that it was the FBI who falsified an email (redacted) to facilitate a bogus FISA warrant in a bogus CI investigation. I bet you the (redacted) is angry as hell about this fiasco. Let us also not forget that it was the FBI who went after a retired American general who had been selected as the National Security Advisor for a President they did not like because he would discover the bogus CI investigation carried out by the FBI. This is unconscionable.

Therefore, intelligence organizations often avoid working with the FBI, especially when it comes to U.S. persons. The FBI's actions in this case are just the examples we know about. Are there other instances where the FBI has done similar things regarding U.S. persons? The answer is probably yes.

Of particular interest is this statement in the ProPublica article: "The Trump supporters who stormed the Capitol may have also benefited from hiding in plain sight. They were not hardcore extremists with a well-developed project such as a bombing or an assassination, the kind of threat FBI agents monitor with intercepts and informants and in chatrooms. Instead, they may have coalesced behind a few leaders with a vague plan who took advantage of weak defenses and mob mentality." [200]

This whole statement could have been: "There is nothing indicating that the January 6th event was planned in any way, it was likely just a spontaneous outburst of frustration directed at a government which has lost the faith of many Americans for all the lies we have been caught in in the last several years."

But O'Conner in the same ProPublica article reveals exactly where the mind of the FBI is regarding civil liberties and what they want to do when he states - "Sometimes you miss things because they aren't there to catch. It is difficult when you have a group doing protected First Amendment activity. You must walk a tightrope. In this case, there may have been nothing to pick up. No concrete plot." [201]

Miss things that are not there? What does that mean? Walk a tight rope? Why?

I would think that since you swore an oath to support the U.S. Constitution as your first act as a federal agent this should be easy for you. Unless it isn't easy because you deliberately get out over the line and are worried about being caught on a regular basis.

It is an easy question everyone who has taken an oath should be able to answer. "Have you ever knowingly and willingly violated your oath?" Simple. If the answer is yes, then they should be fired or resign. No exceptions. Gone are the days of the Untouchables. Gone are the days possibly when these people would put their oath above themselves.

According to the ProPublica article — "Federal agencies closely monitor discussions on extremist platforms. But the senior FBI official said he was unaware of any hard intelligence —

such as operational details — about plans to storm the Capitol." 202 That's because there were none. At least on our side and as far as we know.

Government Transparency

I believe the real problem with the FBI, the U.S. government in general, is they cover up their mistakes. In the military we have a saying. Bad news only gets worse over time.

It is one thing to cover up a mistake when it applies to a foreign government. It is another thing to cover up a mistake regarding the American people. The problem is not just the abuse of power, it is the refusal to admit their mistakes. Concealing mistakes and making American citizens do their own investigations to uncover government mistakes has given rise to distrust with the American people. And today, nothing stays secret for long. And it should not stay a secret when if we are to live in a free society.

The 2020 NCTC Domestic Terrorism Conference highlighted this as a concern with the terminology used (with regard to domestic terrorism) when they recommended: **"The U.S. Government needs to find a way to increase public trust by being transparent with the public about how DT definitions are derived, defined, and used; and We (the U.S. government) can undermine the public trust by failing to be transparent or clear about terms—how the U.S. Government uses terms, what we mean by them, and how that may differ from the public's intuitive understanding of DT."** 203 But this is not just about "terms," the language they use. It is about the who, what, when, where and why of their efforts regarding domestic extremism.

It is with a very heavy heart that I write this report. Many of the issues and concerns raised in this report regarding the FBI and the policies and procedures may seem heavy-handed. They are meant to be so in-order-to articulate the dilemma the FBI is in from their past mistakes not to mention the pressure they feel to solve problems that they cannot solve (i.e., lone actors, suffering from mental health issues and radicalized to violence).

I believe the people in the FBI are moral, ethical, and loyal guardians of the constitution just like me. My hope is to help bring to light the problems the FBI has regarding collecting intelligence on American citizens and hopefully help the Congress, Department of Justice and the FBI begin to see how they are perceived from the outside by regular Americans who just love our country and constitution.

We still believe we are the greatest country that has ever existed in the history of mankind, and we are willing to do whatever it takes to protect it from all enemies.

Because of love of our country and the U.S. Constitution, I guess some people may consider me an extremist. I believe in the constitution. I am sworn to God to defend it. I have made promises to my family to defend them. I am sworn to not only support the constitution, but to defend it.

In my travels across the Commonwealth of Virginia, I often met Virginian's who were very fearful of the federal government getting ready to seize their guns or rob them of their liberty. Some of them were in the militias throughout Virginia. All but a few were nothing more than patriotic Americans who had or were losing their faith in their government. But I knew something they did not. The FBI was not looking at them unless they were planning violence. But they did not believe me no matter how much I tried to tell them.

To try and reduce their fears of the federal government I proposed to several that their militia or 2nd Amendment group take up the following credo. My hope was that it would reduce their fears.

> We believe uncompromisingly in our unalienable right to self-defense and our responsibility to protect our communities from all enemies foreign and domestic. We denounce all forms of violence as a method of political change. We will not tolerate those who seek to take advantage of peaceful 1st Amendment activities to instigate violence. We will report anyone who is planning to carry out unlawful violent activities. We renounce all forms of racism or racial animus. We reject the idea that any race or ethnicity is intellectually, morally, or culturally superior to any other. We utterly reject the idea that there is a secret cabal controlling the U.S. government.

Many people laugh when I state in this credo that there is no secret cabal controlling the U.S. government, but it needs to be said because of the excuse the federal government may potentially use to spy on them if they believe this type of conspiracy. I don't know if any of them adopted it, but I hope so.

Conclusion

Many people will think me naive to believe that we can come back from the brink which we appear to be on. But I believe in the American people. I believe that we can be better than this.

This report has been put through the government pre-publication process to ensure that no classified information is inadvertently revealed. I swore and oath to defend the U.S. Constitution and I do not think leakers are abiding by their oath if they do not bring their concerns to their leadership through lawful means.

I do not believe fulfilling my oath of protecting the constitution is extremist. It is an obligation. Everything in this report was brought to the attention of my government bosses before my departure from NCTC and will be provided to government officials in hopes of bringing our country back together again.

I have concerns over the political rhetoric which is I believe is influencing government policy and procedures which threaten our constitution and are eroding our unalienable rights enshrined in the constitution and Bill of Rights.

More than anything I feel the threat to our country stems from the government concealing from the American people it's mistakes. Americans are very forgiving if you are honest and transparent, but we are unforgiving when you lie to us and cheat us.

Transparency is the only possible way to restore faith and confidence with the American people. Most people, virtually all people, who work at the FBI are patriotic Americans. However, when activities are carried out that are not in line with our American values, or mistakes or poor decisions result in unconstitutional activities being carried out against American citizens, we must default to being transparent. Today things cannot remain hidden forever and the more our government tries to cover up their mistakes, the worse it gets.

The real cause of the January 6th events is the growing distrust of the government by many Americans caused by a lack of transparency and an exaggeration of the threats we face by government officials either willfully or out of ignorance of the facts and leaders of federal agencies for political and budgetary purposes, pure and simple.

This lack of transparency is used by media, politicians, bloggers, foreign enemies, and conspiracy nut cases to increase the hyperbolic rhetoric in our political discourse.

No one benefits more from this than our real enemies such as China, Russia and Iran. I believe our own FBI has unwittingly fallen under the influence of foreign active measures because they are amplifying these imagined threats because it suits their budgetary purposes.

We must do better.

We must, or the enemy wins.

End Notes

[1] History.com, Ruby Ridge, https://www.history.com/topics/1990s/ruby-ridge (Jan 2018)
[2] History.com, Waco Siege, https://www.history.com/topics/1990s/waco-siege (Dec 2017)
[3] Ibid.
[4] Ibid.
[5] Ibid.
[6] EVALUATION OF THE HANDLING OF THE BRANCH DAVIDIAN STAND-OFF IN WACO, TEXAS FEBRUARY 28 TO APRIL 19, 1993, US Department of Justice Archives, https://www.justice.gov/archives/publications/waco/evaluation-handling-branch-davidian-stand-waco-texas-february-28-april-19-1993 (1993)
[7] History.com, Waco Siege, https://www.history.com/topics/1990s/waco-siege (Dec 2017)
[8] FBI Reverses its stand on Waco, washingtonpost.com, https://www.washingtonpost.com/wp-srv/national/daily/aug99/davidians26.htm (1999)
[9] History.com, Timothy McVeigh, https://www.history.com/this-day-in-history/mcveigh-convicted-for-oklahoma-city-bombing, accessed May 23, 2021
[10] ABC News, PrimeTime: McVeigh's Own Words, https://abcnews.go.com/Primetime/story?id=132158&page=1 (Jan 6, 2006) accessed May 23, 2021
[11] ProPublica, Domestic Terrorism: A More Urgent Threat, but Weaker Laws, https://www.propublica.org/article/domestic-terrorism-a-more-urgent-threat-but-weaker-laws, Sebastian Rotella (Jan. 7, 2021)
[12] Ibid.
[13] Ibid.
[14] House Oversight and Reform Subcommittee on Civil Rights and Civil Liberties, https://www.c-span.org/video/?461379-1/hearing-federal-response-white-supremacy (June 4th, 2019)
[15] Ibid.
[16] Ibid.
[17] Ibid.
[18] Ibid.
[19] Ibid.
[20] Ibid.
[21] Hearing on Federal Response to White Supremacy, https://www.c-span.org/video/?461379-1/hearing-federal-response-white-supremacy , June 4, 2019 ((approx. timestamp 1:13:00)
[22] House Oversight and Reform Subcommittee on Civil Rights and Civil Liberties, https://www.c-span.org/video/?461379-1/hearing-federal-response-white-supremacy (June 4th, 2019)
[23] Ibid.
[24] National Archives, Executive Order 12333--United States intelligence activities, https://www.archives.gov/federal-register/codification/executive-order/12333.html
[25] Ibid.
[26] CSIS, Seth Jones, The War Comes Home: The Evolution of Domestic Terrorism in the United States https://www.csis.org/analysis/war-comes-home-evolution-domestic-terrorism-united-states (October 22, 2020)
[27] Ibid.
[28] Ibid.
[29] Ibid.
[30] Ibid.
[31] Ibid.
[32] Ibid.
[33] CSIS, Seth Jones, The Military, Police, and the Rise of Terrorism in the United States, https://www.csis.org/analysis/military-police-and-rise-terrorism-united-states (April 12, 2021)
[34] Ibid.
[35] Ibid.
[36] Ibid.
[37] ODNI, National Counterterrorism Center – Domestic Terrorism Conference Report,

[37] https://www.dni.gov/index.php/nctc-newsroom/item/2105-nctc-s-domestic-terrorism-conference-report, January 2020
[38] Ibid.
[39] ProPublica, Domestic Terrorism: A More Urgent Threat, but Weaker Laws, https://www.propublica.org/article/domestic-terrorism-a-more-urgent-threat-but-weaker-laws (January 7, 2021)
[40] FBI Records: The Vault, https://vault.fbi.gov/cointel-pro
[41] NPR, COINTELPRO and the History of Domestic Spying, https://www.npr.org/templates/story/story.php?storyId=5161811
[42] The Federal Bureau of Investigation's Compliance with the Attorney General's Investigative Guidelines (Redacted) Special Report from September 2005 Office of the Inspector General, https://oig.justice.gov/reports/federal-bureau-investigations-compliance-attorney-generals-investigative-guidelines
[43] ODNI, National Counterterrorism Center – Domestic Terrorism Conference Report, https://www.dni.gov/index.php/nctc-newsroom/item/2105-nctc-s-domestic-terrorism-conference-report, January 2020
[44] Ibid.
[45] Ibid.
[46] Ibid.
[47] Ibid.
[48] Ibid.
[49] Ibid.
[50] Ibid.
[51] Ibid.
[52] Ibid.
[53] The Federal Bureau of Investigation's Compliance with the Attorney General's Investigative Guidelines (Redacted) Special Report from September 2005 Office of the Inspector General, https://oig.justice.gov/reports/federal-bureau-investigations-compliance-attorney-generals-investigative-guidelines
[54] Ibid.
[55] BuzzFeed News, WATCHING THE WATCHMEN, Ken Bensinger and Jessica Garrison, https://www.buzzfeednews.com/article/kenbensinger/michigan-kidnapping-gretchen-whitmer-fbi-informant
[56] Audit of the Federal Bureau of Investigation's Management of its Confidential Human Source Validation Processes, November 2019, https://oig.justice.gov/reports/2019/a20009.pdf
[57] Ibid.
[58] Ibid.
[59] Ibid.
[60] Ibid.
[61] Ibid.
[62] Ibid.
[63] Ibid.
[64] Ibid.
[65] Ibid.
[66] Ibid.
[67] Ibid.
[68] Ibid.
[69] Ibid.
[70] Ibid.
[71] Ibid.
[72] Ibid.
[73] Ibid.
[74] Ibid.

[75] Ibid.
[76] Ibid.
[77] Ibid.
[78] Ibid.
[79] Ibid.
[80] Ibid.
[81] Ibid.
[82] Ibid.
[83] Ibid.
[84] Ibid.
[85] Ibid.
[86] Ibid.
[87] Ibid.
[88] Ibid.
[89] Ibid.
[90] US Supreme Court, Brady v. Maryland, 373 U.S. 83 (1963), https://supreme.justia.com/cases/federal/us/373/83/
[91] Audit of the Federal Bureau of Investigation's Management of its Confidential Human Source Validation Processes, November 2019, https://oig.justice.gov/reports/2019/a20009.pdf
[92] Ibid.
[93] Ibid.
[94] Ibid.
[95] Ibid.
[96] Ibid.
[97] Ibid.
[98] Ibid.
[99] Senate Judiciary Committee, March 2, 2021, FBI Director Christopher Wray testified before the Senate Judiciary Committee on the January 6 attack on the U.S. Capitol
https://www.c-span.org/video/?509033-1/fbi-director-christopher-wray-testifies-january-6-capitol-attack
[100] Ibid.
[101] Ibid.
[102] Ibid.
[103] S.894 - Domestic Terrorism Prevention Act of 2019, https://www.congress.gov/bill/116th-congress/senate-bill/894/text?q=%7B%22search%22%3A%5B%22white+supremacy%22%5D%7D&r=1&s=2
[104] Ibid.
[105] Ibid.
[106] Ibid.
[107] Ibid.
[108] Ibid.
[109] Senate Judiciary Committee, March 2, 2021, FBI Director Christopher Wray testified before the Senate Judiciary Committee on the January 6 attack on the U.S. Capitol
https://www.c-span.org/video/?509033-1/fbi-director-christopher-wray-testifies-january-6-capitol-attack
[110] Ibid.
[111] Ibid.
[112] Ibid.
[113] Ibid.
[114] Ibid.
[115] Ibid.

[116] Ibid.
[117] Ibid.
[118] Ibid.

[119] Ibid.

[120] THE GEORGE WASHINGTON UNIVERSITY, "This is Our House!" A Preliminary Assessment of the Capitol Hill Siege Participants, Program on Extremism, March 2021, https://extremism.gwu.edu/sites/g/files/zaxdzs2191/f/This-Is-Our-House.pdf

[121] Senate Judiciary Committee, March 2, 2021, FBI Director Christopher Wray testified before the Senate Judiciary Committee on the January 6 attack on the U.S. Capitol
https://www.c-span.org/video/?509033-1/fbi-director-christopher-wray-testifies-january-6-capitol-attack

[122] Ibid.

[123] Ibid.

[124] Ibid.

[125] Ibid.

[126] Ibid.

[127] Ibid.

[128] Ibid.

[129] Ibid.

[130] Ibid.

[131] Ibid.

[132] Ibid.

[133] Ibid.

[134] Ibid.

[135] Ibid.

[136] Ibid.

[137] Ibid.

[138] Ibid.

[139] Ibid.

[140] Ibid.

[141] FBI Releases 2020 Hate Crime Statistics, August 30, 2021, https://www.fbi.gov/news/pressrel/press-releases/fbi-releases-2020-hate-crime-statistics?utm_campaign=email-Immediate&utm_medium=email&utm_source=national-press-releases&utm_content=%5B1237754%5D-%2Fnews%2Fpressrel%2Fpress-releases%2Ffbi-releases-2020-hate-crime-statistics

[142] Ibid.

[143] Ibid.

[144] Ibid.

[145] Ibid.

[146] Ibid.

[147] Ibid.

[148] Ibid.

[149] Ibid.

[150] Ibid.

[151] DHS, Office of Intelligence and Analysis, Rightwing Extremism: Current Economic and Political Climate Fueling Resurgence in Radicalization and Recruitmenthttps://fas.org/irp/eprint/rightwing.pdf (April 7, 2009)

[152] (U) Intelligence Community Authorized Classification and Control Markings Register and Manual
Volume 5, Edition 1 (Version 5.1) (Effective: 30 December 2011) Administrative Update, 30 March 2012
Controlled Access Program Coordination Office (CAPCO) Washington, DC 20511
https://www.dni.gov/files/documents/FOIA/Public_CAPCO_Register%20and%20Manual%20v5.1.pdf

[153] Ibid.

[154] (U) Office of the Director of National Intelligence, Classification Guide (ODNI CG), Includes Administrative Update September 30, 2014, Version 2.1, Supersedes 3 July 2012, Version 2.0, j(b)(3) I OPI: DNI-CLASSIFICATION
https://www.dni.gov/files/documents/FOIA/DF-2015-00044%20(Doc1).pdf

[155] Ibid.

[156] DHS, Office of Intelligence and Analysis, Rightwing Extremism: Current Economic and Political Climate Fueling

Resurgence in Radicalization and Recruitment https://fas.org/irp/eprint/rightwing.pdf (April 7, 2009)

[157] Ibid.

[158] Ibid.

[159] Christopher Wray, Director, Federal Bureau of Investigation, Statement Before the House Homeland Security Committee, Washington, D.C., September 17, 2020, Worldwide Threats to the Homeland, Statement for the Record https://www.fbi.gov/news/testimony/worldwide-threats-to-the-homeland-091720

[160] Ibid.

[161] Ibid.

[162] Ibid.

[163] Ibid.

[164] Ibid.

[165] Department of Homeland Security, Homeland Threat Assessment, https://www.dhs.gov/sites/default/files/publications/2020_10_06_homeland-threat-assessment.pdf (October 2020)

[166] Ibid.

[167] Ibid.

[168] Ibid.

[169] Ibid.

[170] Ibid.

[171] Ibid.

[172] Ibid.

[173] Ibid.

[174] Ibid.

[175] Ibid.

[176] DHS, DHS Creates New Center for Prevention Programs and Partnerships and Additional Efforts to Comprehensively Combat Domestic Violent Extremism, https://www.dhs.gov/news/2021/05/11/dhs-creates-new-center-prevention-programs-and-partnerships-and-additional-efforts (May 11, 2021)

[177] Ibid.

[178] Ibid.

[179] U.S. Senate Appropriations Committee, Domestic Violent Extremism in America, https://www.appropriations.senate.gov/hearings/domestic-violent-extremism-in-america (May 12, 2021)

[180] Ibid.

[181] Ibid.

[182] Ibid.

[183] Examining the U.S. Capitol Attack: A review of the security, planning, and response failures on January 6, Staff Report, https://www.rules.senate.gov/imo/media/doc/Jan%206%20HSGAC%20Rules%20Report.pdf

[184] Ibid.

[185] Ibid.

[186] Ibid.

[187] Ibid.

[188] Ibid.

[189] Ibid.

[190] Ibid.

[191] Ibid.

[192] Ibid.

[193] Ibid.

[194] Ibid.

[195] ProPublica, Domestic Terrorism: A More Urgent Threat, but Weaker Laws, https://www.propublica.org/article/domestic-terrorism-a-more-urgent-threat-but-weaker-laws, Sebastian Rotella Jan. 7, 2021

[196] Ibid.

[197] Ibid.
[198] Ibid.
[199] Ibid.
[200] Ibid.
[201] Ibid.
[202] Ibid.
[203] ODNI, National Counterterrorism Center – Domestic Terrorism Conference Report, https://www.dni.gov/index.php/nctc-newsroom/item/2105-nctc-s-domestic-terrorism-conference-report, January 2020